beat
panic & anxiety

the complete guide
to understanding and tackling anxiety disorders

JOHN ILLMAN
SERIES EDITOR **RITA CARTER**

First published as *Use Your Brain to Beat Panic and Anxiety* in Great
Britain in 2004 by Cassell Illustrated, a division of
Octopus Publishing Group Limited, 2–4 Heron Quays, London, E14 4JP.

This edition published in 2006 by Cassell Illustrated.

Text © 2004 John Illman
Design and layout © 2004 Octopus Publishing Group Limited

The moral right of John Illman to be identified as the author of this work
has been asserted in accordance with the Copyright, Designs and
Patents Act, 1988.

A CIP catalogue record for this book is available from the British Library.

ISBN-13: 978-1-844035-07-6
ISBN-10: 1-844035-07-7
Design by DW Design, Printed at Toppan, China

Author's acknowledgements

I am extremely grateful to the following who gave me their wisdom,
expertise and time, especially as the deadline loomed and the title of
this book assumed a dreadful irony. My son James, a psychologist, who
helped with the research; Rita, the series editor, for entrusting me with
another title in the series; Joanne Wilson my editor at Cassell Illustrated,
for her professionalism and for not panicking when she had every right
to, and Dr Kate Cavanagh. To Stuart Toole, for reading the CBT text,
thank you to Professor Edzard Ernst, a doctor for whom I have the
highest regard, for reading the complementary medicine text; thanks
to Dr David Taylor for reading the text and providing advice about drug
therapy; thanks to Professor Isaac Marks who introduced me to the
concept of computerized cognitive behaviour therapy at a lecture in
2003; thank you to the many patients who gave their time to talk to
James and myself about their experiences of anxiety and panic; thank
you No Panic for your help and for providing us with people to interview.
Thank you to Rhian Thomas for providing background information about
prescribing trends, thanks also to Liz, Chris and other members of the
family for their support.

beat
panic & anxiety

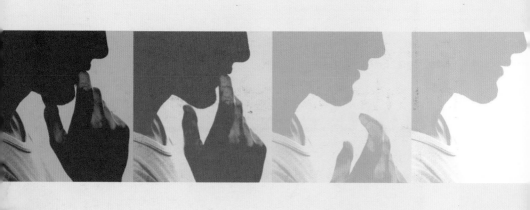

Contents

Introduction

Most people tend to think of anxiety as something that comes and goes, according to circumstances at any one time. Many people are also lucky enough to be left without long-term problems produced by anxiety; however, this is not true for everyone. In some cases, anxiety does not go away – and without treatment it can become progressively worse. Or else, the periods of anxiety become increasingly intense and concentrated in the form of panic attacks or phobias. Sometimes these very physical feelings become disabling – which is what people mean when they refer to "disorders".

In fact, all too often anxiety becomes chronic. Fearful of the anxiety itself, the sufferer becomes caught up in a vicious circle that is hard to break, and in which one anxiety disorder can quickly become two. For example, a panic attack (a sudden devastating bout of acute anxiety) in a specific situation can lead to agoraphobia (fear of leaving a place of safety). In turn, this can trigger depression. Sometimes even people not usually prone to anxiety find themselves caught up in their own negative cycle, where everyday worries become problematic and hinder relationships or work. This book is for both the debilitated sufferer and those with less severe anxiety problems.

The only path to freedom from anxiety is treatment, but acknowledging the problem and taking action is not always easy. Though anxiety disorders are the most common kind of mental health problem, many sufferers do not seek help or advice for fear they will be seen as weak or feeble.

So what is the best way forward? There is no "best treatment" – only best treatments for specific individuals. This book shows you how to access the resources you need – both from within yourself, and in the form of therapy options – to find the right treatment for you. Tackling an anxiety disorder is not just a matter of undergoing psychological treatment or taking drugs. It is a way of life. In the long term, when your formal treatment is complete, your lifestyle can be just as important as psychological support or medication.

Part One: Panic and anxiety, explains the signs and symptoms of the different types of anxiety disorder and looks at pointers to potential problems as well as identifying clear signs and symptoms. It looks at the risk factors associated with anxiety, the role of stress and what happens in the brain during an anxiety disorder. Part One also introduces the different types of disorders, it looks at the role of diet and exercise in keeping anxiety at bay and includes a review of the role of complementary medicine in treating anxiety disorders.

Part Two: Cognitive behaviour therapy, provides an introduction to a highly successful psychological treatment, which can be pursued either on its own or in combination with drugs. Dubbed "the thinking man's psychotherapy", CBT focuses predominantly on the here and now rather than on the distant past history of the client/patient. We describe revolutionary CBT computer programmes that could increasingly offer treatment to hundreds and thousands of people. Computerized CBT is challenging the traditional idea that contact with another human is a prerequisite of successful treatment. Some people don't actually want to be face to face with someone while recounting personal and distressing experiences and feelings.

Part Three: Resources, provides details of the different drugs available, including their benefits and side effects, for you to weigh up the pros and cons of the different approaches. You may decide drug treatment is not for you, but this section lists the common drugs prescribed in severe cases. Finally, we include contacts for further information and a reading list – everything you need to help you use your brain to beat your problem.

Part One
Panic and anxiety

1 Understanding panic and anxiety

"In trouble to be troubled is to have your trouble doubled."

Daniel Defoe, *The Further Adventures of Robinson Crusoe,* **1719**

Anxious? Well, doesn't everyone get anxious?

Exams, public speaking, a first date, a critical presentation, children starting school or leaving home, a job interview – all these things make us anxious. Even supposedly relaxing activities, like going on holiday, can cause anxiety. These responses are normal, even desirable: short-term anxiety is part of the coping mechanism which helps prime us for action, take stock and react to danger. It can bring out the best in us – even if it does make us feel physically sick. Many star actors and performers experience acute anxiety before going on stage.

Fortunately, few people react in such an extreme way as Richard Villar. Recalling his first parachute jump as a military surgeon in the British Special Air Services (SAS), he writes: "The parachute jump instructor (PJI) barely gave me time to think further. The moment the red light glowed to one side of the exit, he pulled open the door. When that happens, your insides work overtime. I was terrified. My legs shook as I felt the slow trickle of urine down the inside of my thigh. Then the light changed from red to green. 'Go', shouted the PJI at the top of his lungs…Before I had time to think, I had plunged through the buffeting slipstream into the quieter air beyond. Slowly, hesitantly, I opened my eyes and looked upwards. Thank God. There above me was the perfect hemisphere of my open parachute. The relief was overwhelming."[1]

This kind of transient anxiety can be incredibly dramatic, but it is not harmful. In contrast, the kind of anxiety which threatens physical and mental health can be persistent and can be excessive. However, no clear division exists between healthy concern and potentially disabling anxiety. The doctor cannot judge the severity of your anxiety on a scale of one to ten. Only you know how bad it is. A guide such as the one opposite would help doctors distinguish "normal" anxiety from a clinical anxiety disorder.

Signs and symptoms of anxiety

An anxiety disorder may be indicated if a person has experienced some of the following symptoms more often than not during the past six months (when triggered by anxious feelings):

■ Restlessness or feeling on edge

■ Tiring quickly

■ Inability to control feelings of anxiety

■ Difficulty concentrating or inability to focus on anything

■ Short temper/frustration/irritability

■ Muscle tension

■ Disturbed sleep patterns (difficulty falling or staying asleep or restless sleep).

"I stopped giving dinner parties because I just couldn't bear the anxiety about getting everything ready in time. It got so bad that I'd start worrying days before the event."

Understanding Anxiety, **Mind, 2002**

Alternatively, if a person feels anxious most or all of the time over a prolonged period in the absence of any of the above additional factors, this may also indicate the presence of an anxiety disorder.

The above is not a substitute for professional medical opinion or advice. You should consult your doctor if you believe you suffer from an anxiety disorder.

When anxiety stops being healthy

Registering alarm about a threat is normal; but a panic attack is something else entirely. If you have never experienced an attack, then try and imagine quietly watching TV, waiting for a bus or something similarly "everyday". Imagine then experiencing sudden, intense fear and feelings of impending doom, shortness of breath and chest pain. This is a panic attack as described in the internationally acclaimed psychiatrists' "bible", published by the American Psychiatric Association, the *Diagnostic and Statistical Manual of Mental Disorders*. Other anxiety disorders include:

Agoraphobia: Avoidance of places or situations from which escape might be difficult or embarrassing, or in which help may not be available in the event of a panic attack or panic-like symptoms; usually accompanied by feelings of anxiety or depression.

Specific phobia: Intense dread or fear of a particular object or situation such as a snake, insects, the sight of blood, flying or taking examinations. The distinction between phobia and normal fear is that the former is disproportionate to the danger. Many people have mild phobias, which don't significantly affect their lives, but for some, phobias can be severely disabling.

Social phobias: Anxiety in public or performance situations.

Obsessive-compulsive disorder (OCD): Anxious, repetitive thoughts and rituals beyond an individual's control. Obsessions may cause pronounced anxiety and stress. Compulsive acts, like repeated hand washing, can have a reassuring, comforting effect, in the short term, but they are often followed by intense anxiety.

Post-traumatic stress disorder (PTSD): reliving extreme trauma like a major accident or war or sexual assault can cause severe, emotion-numbing anxiety. An existing anxiety or depressive disorder may increase the risk of PTSD. Acute stress disorder produces similar symptoms to post-traumatic stress disorder in the aftermath of an extremely traumatic event.

We will be looking at each of these in more detail, after examining the factors which make some people more vulnerable to anxiety disorders than others.

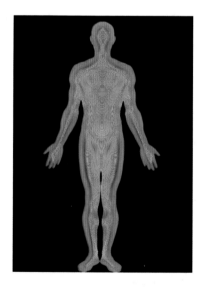

The symptoms of anxiety can be physical, but the causes are often external and internal factors specific to the individual. External and internal triggers to anxiety will also affect people differently.

Anxiety checklist

Are you A) Feeling tense or anxious or B) Worrying about a lot of things?
If you answered yes to either of the above, continue below:

1. Are you experiencing symptoms of arousal and anxiety?

2. Have you experienced fear unexpectedly or for no apparent reason? eg.

■ Fear of dying

■ Fear of losing control

■ Pounding heart

■ Sweating

■ Trembling or shaking

■ Chest pains or difficulty breathing

■ Feeling dizzy, lightheaded or faint

■ Numbness or tingling sensations

■ Feelings of unreality

■ Nausea

3. Have you experienced fear/ anxiety in specific situations? eg.

■ Leaving familiar places

■ Travelling alone, eg. by train, car, plane

■ Crowds/confined spaces/public places

4. Experienced fear/anxiety in social situations? eg.

■ Speaking in front of others

■ Social events

■ Eating in front of others

■ Worrying a lot about what others think, being self-conscious? [2]

Replies of "yes" to A, B and 1, recurring regularly, and "no" to 2, 3 and 4, may indicate generalized anxiety disorder (G.A.D.).

Replies of "yes" to 1 and 2 may indicate panic disorder.

Replies of "yes" to 2 and 3 may indicate agoraphobia.

Replies of "yes" to 3 and 4 may indicate social phobia.

The checklist to the left is not a substitute for professional medical opinion or advice. You should consult your doctor if you believe you suffer from an anxiety disorder.

Why are some people affected by extreme anxiety?

You may know what makes you anxious without necessarily knowing why. Fear and anxiety affect us all differently. Some people, quite simply, have a low threshold for anxiety – their reaction to a particular anxiety-provoking situation may be out of all proportion to its magnitude. So what makes them especially vulnerable? A key factor is the level of control we have over our lives.

The US psychologist Suzanne Kobasa developed the "hardy personality" theory after finding that some executives share three characteristics which make them "significantly less likely to fall ill, either mentally or physically". The characteristics are tied into the three "c" s below:

1. **Commitment:** These people totally involve themselves in what they do – putting the maximum effort into life, work, relationships etc.

2. **Control:** People with hardy personalities believe and act as if they can influence events.

3. **Challenge:** Considering change as an opportunity for personal development is a key attribute.

Another psychologist, Julian Rotter, developed the "Locus of Control" theory which assumes we have either an external or internal locus (point) of control. "Internals" believe they can control events and dictate the course of their own lives. "Externals" think of themselves as people with limited control whose lives are predominantly determined by others. They are thought to be more susceptible to emotional disorders than internals according to his theory. Inevitably, the way we perceive or think of ourselves affects the way we feel and behave. Cognitive behaviour therapy (CBT), (see page 88), is designed to change the way we think and feel and behave. This involves acknowledging the causes of our anxieties and fears – which is not always easy. Ignored or unacknowledged, anxiety can take control of our lives. Conversely, if it is acknowledged it can be seen as a warning – as a signal to take stock and subsequently resolve a particular problem.

Try the questionnaire opposite, developed by Cary Cooper, an international authority on stress, to see if you are an "internal" or an "external". If you are an "external" your CBT treatment may take a different form than if you are an "internal". Your triggers to stress may be related to things which are beyond your control, and in this instance it is important to develop a programme which enables you to acknowledge this. Even if you are an internal this does not mean that you will not be stressed; in fact your stress can have far-reaching consequences. The extremely organized and calm individual is open to extreme stress when something unforseen happens – such as a trauma at home or in relationships. Nobody can avoid stress and nor should they try. CBT – the subject of Part Two – is about acknowledging and identifying stressors, and learning that if we understand our own unique make-up we can avoid stress becoming harmful.

Are you in control?

Circle the number that best reflects your attitudes, then add up your total
score. Score **0–25** = internal, **26–35** = internal/external, **36–50** = external

Strongly disagree	**1**
Disagree	**2**
Uncertain	**3**
Agree	**4**
Strongly Agree	**5**

Our society is run by a few people with enormous power and there is not
much the ordinary person can do about it.

1 2 3 4 5

One's success is determined by being in the "right place at the right time".

1 2 3 4 5

There will always be industrial relations disputes no matter how hard people
try to prevent them or no matter how hard they try to take an active role in
union activities.

1 2 3 4 5

Politicians are inherently self-interested and inflexible. It is impossible to
change the course of politics.

1 2 3 4 5

What happens in life is predestined.

1 2 3 4 5

People are inherently lazy, so there is no real point in spending too
much time in changing them.

1 2 3 4 5

I do not see a direct connection between the way and how hard I work
and the assessments of my performance that others arrive at.

1 2 3 4 5

Leadership qualities are primarily inherited.

1 2 3 4 5

I am fairly certain that luck and chance play a crucial role in life.

1 2 3 4 5

Even though some people try to control events – taking part in political or social
affairs, in reality we are subject to forces we cannot comprehend or control. [3]

1 2 3 4 5

Why are some people more "in control" than others?

There is no simple answer – and probably no single answer for any one of us. It depends upon the interplay between many things such as genetic make-up, personality type, an individual's coping skills, environmental influences, personal experience, age and social supports (friends, relatives, self-help groups and health-care professionals). A certain combination of factors might point to a tendency to anxiety disorders. It may be hard to establish which aspects of someone's life are responsible for a specific anxiety disorder, or if there is one single trigger. Some people, for example, seem to have a genetic predisposition to anxiety disorders, but it is impossible to disentangle genetic factors from environmental ones. At any one time many different influences affect the way we feel, including everything from the trauma of major events like bereavement, redundancy and divorce to persistent everyday "minor" hassles. These can have major consequences, and often we have little power to control them. For example, you may be intensely irritated by a particular part of your daily working routine – yet there might be nothing you can do about it.

In Mary's case (see opposite) we see someone convinced about the origins of her anxiety. Her childhood was blighted by bereavement and problems at school. (Of course, a happy childhood does not guarantee immunity from anxiety.) At the age of 22, Grace Sheppard seemed to have everything – good health, good looks and a loving family. Her marriage to David Sheppard, then an international cricketer and later Bishop of Liverpool, completed a dream picture. Then she became afraid to leave the safety of her own home.[4] She believes a severe attack of chickenpox triggered her agoraphobia. Chickenpox is not known as a "precursor" of anxiety states, but Grace's illness may have brought to the surface a number of anxiety-provoking elements. See page 43 for more on agoraphobia.

Mary's story

 I have a theory that people are born with a predisposition to these things. As a child I also had to cope with bereavement and problems at school. One day, I'd just got off the bus and felt something was terribly wrong. I felt very, very frightened and stood rooted to the spot...It was in the 1950s and no help was available. My parents thought I would grow out of it.

This was my introduction to agoraphobia. My chief hang-up was travelling by train and going up very high buildings. I kept thinking someone was telling me to jump. I hated station platforms. For a long time I couldn't even walk along the road because I felt something was telling me to walk into the traffic.

I was convinced I must have done something to deserve it. I felt unworthy and soiled and like an unexploded bomb just waiting to go off. I became convinced that sooner or later I'd commit some violent crime.

I have a particular vivid memory of a family row over some property. Unfortunately, both my parents died before we had the chance to reconcile our differences. The worst time was when my mother died. I couldn't even get to the funeral. I didn't think anyone would want me there anyway.

I used to feel guilty, and, though I will always carry a burden, I feel differently about things now. I recognize that I'm not 100 per cent perfect and that every human being has faults. I now live in a better family atmosphere and better circumstances and I've been helped by the fact that more information and help has become available – thanks to the media and self- help groups like No Panic.* Hearing other people speak about their experiences makes you realize you're not an outcast.

*see Resources, page 161

Mary, 68, pensioner

Anxiety – what lies beneath?

We have referred in very general terms to risk factors. Examining specific risk factors may help identify the origins of an anxiety disorder. Increased understanding may also boost self-esteem and confidence, which is an important factor as so often people are afraid to ask for help. Key factors which may affect someone's tendency to an anxiety disorder include:

Repressed feelings: Most of us at times push uncomfortable feelings from our minds, to avoid an argument or to keep the peace. There may be embarrassing or worrying things we would rather not talk about, even to partners or close friends. The final decision by many people to talk about something really pressing – say, a fear of cancer – may come only after long, lonely nights of despair. They may want to talk, but fear that doing so will somehow make it seem real, even in the absence of a diagnosis.

Alternatively, as a child you may have been brought up to believe that children should be seen and not heard, and been unable to confide in your parents for fear of being mocked or scolded. As an adult, you may continue to keep your opinions to yourself because old habits really do die hard. Psychoanalysts believe repressing feelings can make us anxious – and it is easy to see how this happens.

Personality types: Your personality may affect your susceptibility to anxiety disorders. Research has found that the level of fear of patients awaiting surgery is less directly linked to the seriousness of the operation than to personality and an individual's style of coping. A traumatic divorce or a life-threatening disease may generate anxiety in even the most robust of individuals – but they may find a way of quickly bouncing back. Linked to personality are our social support mechanisms and our exposure to stress, which vary among personality types.

Coping style: A negative coping style in which an individual sees themselves as "second rate" or "worthless" can quickly become self-perpetuating. Adopting an alternative, positive outlook is not just a matter of "que sera, sera" or "no worries" – if only it were that easy. Positive thinking will only really work if it is built on a secure foundation. This means addressing existing problems by developing effective coping skills; not by comfort-eating, drinking, psychological denial, avoidance and escapism – all things which are all too frequently passed off as relaxing.

In *Relax: Dealing with Stress,* (BBC Books, 1992) Murray Watts and Professor Cary L. Cooper warn: "In the B-movie western, when the hero is in trouble, there is always the 'old trick' that might just work. Unhappily, our schemes for dealing with stress frequently don't work, and, in fact, make our problems much worse. We need to face up to 'the old tricks', our ploys, our distractions, our habits, addictions, excuses. We need to face up to ourselves."

Social support: The decline in traditional support systems – social contact, neighbourhood and family – has left many people feeling helpless or hopeless, without control over their own destiny. How many times do we hear that the world is moving too fast, has become too crowded and is indifferent to basic human needs? The self-help movement is filling the vacuum – to the benefit of many people interviewed for this book. (See Resources.)

Family history: Research suggests anxiety disorders run in families and that fear is encoded in our genes. It is unclear how much of an anxiety-prone family's problems can be attributed to genes and how much to everyday behaviour. A child may develop a spider phobia because he has seen his mother recoil in horror from a spider; not just because of his genes. Whichever is true, a tendency to anxiety disorder certainly runs in families.

Stress: This is a major risk factor and the focus of the next section.

2 The stress factor: living in overdrive

"Stress itself is not a thing; it is our reaction to things. Stress can be defined as our mental, emotional and physical responses to the irritants, challenges and threats – individual and accumulated – in our lives."

Texas Heart Institute, *Heart Owner's Handbook*, **John Wiley and Sons, Inc., 1996**

Stress: a primitive response?

We would probably say we were "afraid" if we were attacked by muggers, and "anxious" if we had financial or marital problems. Our bodies make no such distinction. The stress response to fear and anxiety is often exactly the same. In less than a second the body automatically triggers a number of physical changes in preparation to fight or take flight. This animalistic response was ideal for our primitive ancestors whose exposure to fear and anxiety tended more towards short-term tooth and claw emergencies. It is less well suited for the complexities of twenty-first-century life, with all its long-term problems. Most of us face the same situations, the same family, the same colleagues, the same pressures and the same stresses, week in, week out. There is nowhere to run, no primitive way out.

The body also makes no distinction between real and irrational, imagined fears. A company boss who mistakenly thinks for months that the board wants to sack him may suffer from prolonged stress. Normally, he would tick over like a car being driven in the right gear, speeding up and slowing down to adjust to traffic conditions. However, his anxiety about his fellow directors makes him more like a family saloon travelling at 50 mph an hour in second gear. There is a limit to how long a car engine will work in the wrong gear and the body is just the same. It breaks down if the hormonal "accelerators" are pressed down hard for too long.

But stress is not all bad. Competitive games can be immensely stressful – as can conducting an orchestra. Stress gives a sharp edge to our performance. This kind of intense short-term stress is what evolution has equipped us to cope with. The body reacts to acute stress by releasing two types of chemical messengers: hormones in the blood and neurotransmitters in the brain. The primary stress hormone, cortisol, is very important in marshalling systems throughout the body, including the heart, lungs, circulation and immune system. Other stress hormones include adrenaline and noradrenaline.

The human performance curve

Stress is essential for our survival. It alerts us to danger, helps us to cope with the demands of daily life and can sharpen our performance. The human performance curve, from Dr Chandra Patel's book *The Complete Guide to Stress Management*, (Vermillion, 1996) emphasizes the importance of balancing the stress in our life.

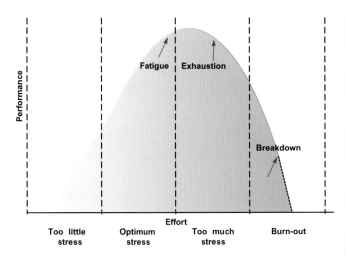

Too little stress: this results in insufficient challenge to achieve a sense of personal accomplishment.

Optimum stress: life is balanced despite its ups and downs, and perfectly manageable.

Too much stress: constant feeling of having to do too much every day, resulting in permanent overdrive and emotional and physical exhaustion – and finally burn-out.

Measuring the impact of stressful situations

Researchers have tried to measure the stress factors of different situations – with controversial results. Thomas H. Holmes and Richard R. Rahe of the University of Washington compiled a list of about 40 stressful situations or "life events", such as the death of a partner, marital separation, a change to a different line of work and sexual problems.[5] Each was allocated a score. For example, 100 in the case of the death of a spouse; 73 for divorce; and 23 for trouble with the boss. Someone scoring a total of more than 300 was estimated to have an 80 per cent chance of developing a stress-related illness.

This scale is widely used, but has obvious drawbacks. Firstly, it does not take into account day to day stress. Secondly, life events affect different people in different ways. For example, the stress of divorce may have limited impact if a couple has been separated for a long time. Critics say it is not the stressor itself which is important so much as how it is perceived. You may regard an exam as overwhelming or as a mere trifle.

There are many different ways we can interpret what happens to us. For example, the boss praises an employee for an outstanding presentation, while also suggesting ways to improve it. The employee may think: "Those are great ideas. I can make really good use of them." Alternatively, he may think: "That was a really damning criticism. He's out to sack me." Many people jump to the wrong conclusions without examining the evidence for their thoughts and feelings. Of course, negative feelings are sometimes justified – but people with anxiety disorders often have no real basis for their worry and fears.

Gearing up to stress

Stress is widely perceived as something that goes on in our heads – but mind and body function as one. Hans Selye, author of *Stress without Distress*, described the physiological response to stress in three phases – in what he called The General Adaptation Syndrome (GAS). He based this concept on a famous set of experiments subjecting animals to various stressors, including blood loss, exposure to extreme heat and cold and surgical trauma. Irrespective of the stressor, he found the response tended to be similar in all animals. It produces a "fight or flight" response involving a wide range of biological changes to prime the body for action. Human beings experience the same response.

This diagram shows the experience of stress to be a complex relationship between mind and body. While the brain registers fear, the lungs and heart react, making breathing shallow and difficult and the heart beat increases. In panic attack sufferers this can in turn produce more fear – fear of a panic attack itself.

Alarm phase: The heart rate increases to pump more oxygen rich blood to the brain. The breathing rate quickens to meet the demand for more oxygen. The blood is flooded with red blood cells to carry more oxygen into the limbs and brain. Blood-clotting time shortens, making severe bleeding from any wounds less likely. Muscles tighten to prepare the body for "fight or flight". The liver provides fuel for quick energy by releasing sugar and fats into the blood. Perspiration cools the body. Digestion stops to enable blood to be diverted to the brain and muscles – where it is most needed.

Resistance phase: The body gets into a more or less balanced state and develops some resistance to the stressor. The body works to ensure that all its different body systems – from cardiovascular to skeletal – are working in harmony. This phase is of limited duration because this extra work uses vital energy which may be needed for other physiological functions.

Exhaustion: The body's reserves will ultimately be exhausted if the "fight or flight" reaction continues for too long.

Brain

Heart

Lungs

Everyday hassles or source of health-threatening stress?

A grumpy boss, a crowded commuter train, the computer that crashes at a critical time, a sick child or a dependent elderly relative. Most people would classify everyday hassles like these as "minor" compared to the major life events, such as divorce, listed in the Holmes Rahe scale (see page 28). But the late Richard Lazarus, former professor of psychology at the University of California, believed that such hassles are minor only in so much that they do not immediately transform our lives as the death of a partner would. He maintained that routine minor hassles actually have a bigger impact than Holmes and Rahe's life events. Testing out a "daily hassle" measure on 100 people aged between 45 and 65, he and his colleagues found it to be a better pointer to people being at risk of stress-related diseases than the Holmes Rahe scale.

There has been much debate about the links between stress and anxiety and physical disease. Until recently, most doctors treated diseases of body and mind as unrelated, but this traditional split is being re-evaluated. For example, studies have shown clear links between stress and the immune system. Short-term stress increases the number and activity of natural killer cells, the white blood cells that destroy invading bacteria and viruses. But chronic or prolonged stress results in a decrease in the activity of these cells, leaving us vulnerable to infection.

The medical "jury" is still "out" on the links between stress and cancer and stress and heart disease. Critics have accused the medical profession of ignoring or rejecting studies suggesting that psychological and psychosocial factors are involved in the development of cancer. While stress may contribute to the risk of a heart attack, research has not yet shown conclusively that it is a cause of heart disease.[6] Certain heart conditions, however, such as angina (chest pain) can be exacerbated by stress.

Stress check

How often do you experience stress symptoms such as those below? The *Heart Owner's Handbook* recommends keeping a stress diary to note down the times you experience any symptoms. You will, in time, become more adept at identifying your personal stress triggers. Recognizing them can be the first step to controlling them.

- Sudden heart pounding
- Cold clammy hands
- Drumming fingers or tapping foot
- Nervous coughing
- General fatigue
- Frustration
- Dry mouth
- Difficulty breathing
- Muscle aches
- Clenched jaws or other tight facial muscles
- Stiff neck
- Tics at the mouth or eyebrows
- Sudden sweating
- Turning red-faced
- Headaches
- Upset stomach or heartburn
- Sudden anger
- Constant feeling that there isn't enough time
- Sudden tears for no reason
- Sudden sense of impending bad news or doom
- Anxiety
- Depression
- Sudden inability to express yourself
- Overreaction
- Irritability
- Impatience
- Grinding teeth
- Binge drinking
- Binge eating
- Talking too much
- Chain smoking
- Nail biting
- Constant picking at fingernails or face
- Fiddling with/pulling out hair
- Trying to do two or three things at once

Adapted from *Heart Owner's Handbook*, Texas Heart Institute, John Wiley and Sons, 1996

3 The many faces of anxiety

"The problem of anxiety neurosis may be epitomized metaphorically as an over-active 'alarm system'. The anxious patient is so keyed up to the possibility of harm that he is constantly warning himself about potential dangers. The stream of signals flowing through his internal communication system carries one message: *danger*. Almost any stimulus may be sufficient to trip off the warning system and create a 'false alarm'. The consequence of the blizzard of false alarms is that the patient does experience harm – he is in a constant state of anxiety."

Aaron T. Beck, *Cognitive Therapy and the Emotional Disorders,* Penguin Books, 1989

Cause and diagnosis

There are three competing theories about the causes of anxiety:

1. Misguided thinking: This theory is based on the idea that anxiety stems from negative or dysfunctional thoughts and feelings. In turn this affects behaviour. Cognitive behaviour therapy, see Part Two, aims to break this think-feel-behave cycle.

2. Repressed feelings: Freudian psychoanalytic thinking underpins this theory. For example, an employee may be afraid to confront their boss for fear of being made to look small. Their feelings may date back to childhood – and unresolved arguments with parents, which made them think twice about speaking out.

3. Biological abnormalities: This theory advocates the use of drugs to correct chemical imbalances in the brain of an anxious person. Drugs can remove the sharp edges of anxiety, but they can also cause unwanted side effects.

Diagnosing anxiety disorders can be complex. The symptoms of a particular disorder may be hard to unravel, present one day but not the next, and they are sometimes confused with those of other illnesses. Careful diagnosis and identification of a particular anxiety disorder helps the doctor or therapist to summarize what he knows about the particular case, give a prognosis and decide which treatment is the most appropriate. Treatment of phobias may involve gradually introducing the patient to the source of their phobia in graded steps – one step at a time called "exposure therapy". So, someone who fears being alone might be restricted to a few minutes on their own at a time, gradually increasing the time they are alone. Drugs may be an option.

Generalized anxiety disorder (GAD)

Features: GAD causes persistent worry, typically moderate in intensity. The symptoms (see page 13) may ebb and flow, but tend to occur more days than not. Patients describe themselves as being tense, nervous and constantly on edge. They often fear something bad is about to happen, even though there is no reason to think it will. GAD is often called "free floating" because there may be no obvious reason for it, but it may result in worry about health, money, family or work. GAD can be exacerbated by additional stressful events, real or imagined. Simple domestic setbacks such as a cooker breaking down can seem like a major disaster.

Prevalence: GAD is the most commonly diagnosed emotional disorder. One adult in 20 suffers from GAD at any given time (compared with the one in 100 who have panic disorder).[7] GAD is twice as common in women as in men and often begins in the teens.[8]

Related disorders: People with GAD may also suffer from other emotional disorders, such as panic attacks, phobic disorders or depression.

Diagnosis: Because the symptoms of anxiety disorder can be so vague, it may take several consultations with the doctor to confirm the diagnosis. Occasionally an over-active thyroid gland, as well as angina, diabetes, epilepsy or certain types of medicine may cause symptoms similar to GAD.

Treatment options: The long-term outcome after receiving psychological treatment such as cognitive behaviour therapy (CBT) is very often positive, though drug therapy is also an option if such a course fails. Complementary therapy (see pages 69–77) can be successful.

Panic Disorder

Features: A panic attack is a sudden burst of unexplained severe anxiety lasting from a couple of minutes to half an hour or more. It is characterized by severe physical symptoms and catastrophic thoughts such as:

- ■ "I'm going mad."

- ■ "I'm going to die."

- ■ "I'm having a heart attack."

- ■ "I'm losing control."

- ■ "I'm making myself look stupid."

These irrational fears can seem very real because of the accompanying physical symptoms, which may include nausea, excessive sweating, feelings of tingling or numbness, a pounding heart, a feeling of choking or breathlessness and a churning stomach. The speed with which a panic attack takes hold and the wide-ranging nature of the symptoms adds to the overwhelming sense of helplessness and despair. Attacks are often linked to a specific place or activity, such as driving a car, but they can occur totally out of the blue – as in the case of Anne (see page 39). She was quietly watching TV when she had her first attack.

Early treatment can stop panic attacks, which may otherwise occur on a regular basis – i.e., several times a week or even every day.

While panic attacks seem to happen "out of the blue", they often actually evolve in a cyclical pattern (see below). This cycle can take weeks or, in some cases, the cycle is broken before another panic attack occurs.

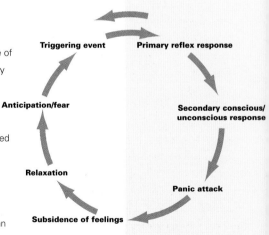

Triggering event

Primary reflex response

Anticipation/fear

Secondary conscious/ unconscious response

Relaxation

Panic attack

Subsidence of feelings

Tom's story

I've just started this new job and I always seem to be worrying. I'm only in my twenties – a time I really expected to enjoy, with money in my pocket, my own flat, and a prestigious job in advertising. Everyone else seems to be on top of things, but I can't get to sleep at night. I keep sweating – which is something else to worry about. Will people notice? Will they ask: what's wrong with him? Sometimes I start trembling and feel my heart pounding.

Having lost one job I'm afraid of losing this one even though the boss has said I've made a very good start. But I keep thinking about all the things that could go wrong – the disasters just waiting to happen. I want everything to be just right and I know I'm likely to get upset if that doesn't happen. I really like people – even though I've got a short fuse – and I really want people to like me. At school I always wanted to be top of the class. Similarly, at university I really wanted to achieve, and I worked really hard. But it was never enough. A close friend has said I'm never really satisfied with what I've got, and spend far too much time looking at the future rather than taking the time out to actually enjoy being in the present.

I haven't been to the doctor. I think this is something I've got to deal with myself. Besides, what's he going to say? He'd probably tick me off for wasting his time and say that if I think I've got a problem, I should see some of his other patients. And I know I'm lucky to be where I am – but I don't feel lucky. I feel really, really tired.

Tom, 25, advertising executive

Causes of panic attacks can be divided into several categories:

Early life: Possible causes range from genetic inheritance to cold and unsupportive families and over-protective parents who make their children feel insecure. Such cases account for only a proportion of the total, however, a stable loving family is no guarantee of immunity.

Early childhood: Exposure to shocking events or abuse or the trauma of an accident or disease can trigger subsequent attacks. For example, asthma-related breathing difficulties in childhood may sensitize the nervous system to changes in blood gas levels. This may increase any probability of full blown panic attacks in later life in the event of anxiety and shallow, rapid breathing (hyperventilation).

Later life: Panic attacks are associated with specific patterns of thought. For example, a minor twitch may provoke catastrophic thoughts about a life-threatening heart attack in someone who is prone to panic attacks. It is easy to see how someone who thinks in this way may come to see themselves as having very little control of their world. Everyday problems become major obstacles, which seem beyond them. They become less and less able to cope and this can have a powerful negative reinforcing effect, affecting self-esteem and confidence. (As we explain later, this is where CBT can help.)

Prevalence: About 2 per cent of men and 5 per cent of women suffer from panic disorder at some stage in their lives.[9]

Related disorders: More than three-quarters of patients diagnosed as having one of the other anxiety disorders also experience panic attacks. Many people prone to panic disorder also suffer from major depression.

Treatment options: CBT, antidepressant therapy and complementary medicine have all been found to work, but treatment varies considerably.

Obsessive-compulsive disorder is sometimes manifested as an overwhelming desire to scrub and wash on an abnormally frequent basis.

Anne's story

 I had my first panic attack at the age of 16 when I was doing my GCSEs. I hated school. One evening around midnight I was watching TV when my heart started racing. I had really strong palpitations and thought I was going to die. The hospital said I'd had a "panic attack". I'd never heard the term before.

I've had them on and off ever since – sometimes daily attacks for weeks on end and then nothing for a few months. No-one could really understand what it's like without having an attack themselves. The adrenaline pumps through the body – it's like an outer body experience. Sometimes I become nauseous and feel as if I'm going to choke. The attacks don't really last very long, but it feels like forever at the time – really frightening.

I live at home with my mum and two sisters and I don't know what I'd do without them. I've got lots of friends, but until very recently I felt unable to go to the pub with them for fear of having a panic attack and ruining their evening. I'm more confident now and happy to go out again.

The idea of turning 30 next year has been a wake-up call. I feel it's time for me to live my life. I'm trying to be positive – to get out there and do things. Listening to other sufferers has helped – as has CBT. I've also tried yoga, relaxation and reflexology, which involves applying pressure to reflex points in the feet and hands. It's said to stimulate the body's own healing system. Deep breathing, visualization techniques* and positive thinking have also helped.

*described on page 77

Anne, 29, healthcare analyst

Obsessive-compulsive disorder (OCD)

Features: The word "obsession" is derived from the Latin, *obsidere*: "to be besieged". OCD results in anxiety-provoking obsessions and compulsive repetitive rituals to relieve the anxiety. People with OCD know they are behaving oddly, but cannot stop. Common OCD-related behaviours include constant washing, counting and rearranging objects in a particular order. A compulsive hand-washer may wear away their skin by constant scrubbing. The legendary tycoon Howard Hughes is reported to have been so obsessed with cleanliness that he disinfected his underpants. But towards the end of his life he became increasingly unwashed and isolated. The American psychiatrist, Judith Rapoport describes Hughes' case history in her book *The Boy Who Couldn't Stop Washing*. She believes his rituals became so time consuming he was unable to carry them out.[10]

Prevalence: Reported to affect between two and three per cent of the population.[11] In most cases, symptoms emerge between the ages of 10 and 30.

Related disorders: Hypochondria (the need to check constantly for signs of bodily illness) and body dysmorphic disorder (the conviction something is wrong with the way one looks) are associated with OCD. Half the reported cases of compulsive hair pulling are also thought to be associated with OCD.

Diagnosis: Many people are driven by a desire, for example, to forever clean their homes or have repeated health checks. However, an essential feature of OCD is its severity. It often takes up an hour a day and disrupts normal life. Symptoms should have lasted for at least two weeks and the patient should recognize at least one of their obsessive or compulsive symptoms as being unreasonable or excessive to make diagnosis possible.

Treatment options: Cognitive therapy and behaviour therapy have all been shown to be effective. In cases where CBT is unavailable/has failed/ is inappropriate, or in severe cases on diagnosis, antidepressants may be appropriate.

A mother's story

Helen's hair was falling out in clumps. We tried to disguise the bald patches by subtle combing and brushing. She was only 13. We saw several doctors, without success, and bought a range of new clothes to make her feel good about herself. Friends even said her new hair looked wonderful, but I was afraid she'd be teased – as she was.

She changed schools and felt excluded and under stress. By this time it was virtually impossible to hide the true extent of the loss and she was being teased. She wanted a wig, but as a last ditch attempt, I suggested scalp stimulation. She suddenly burst into tears and admitted the truth – she'd been pulling out her own hair.

I was relieved because this is what I had suspected. I'd done some research in the local library, discovering that pulling your hair out is a stress-related medical condition called trichotillomania.

We sat down together as a family to discuss things. We said we couldn't shield her from stress and that everyone has to develop coping strategies. We remembered the times when her hair had grown back when she was more relaxed – on holiday, for example. Building up an overall picture helped to pinpoint the times she was most at risk. We started keeping a diary, asking her to record the things that worried her, to encourage her to take responsibility for herself. It was a nerve-wracking time.

Eighteen months later, Helen seems to be fully better – her hair has grown back. We're very thankful but initially we felt very isolated because we got no help from the doctors and felt unable to confide in our friends because Helen might have seen this as a betrayal. I'd have welcomed cognitive therapy if it had been available.

Janet, 50, social worker

Specific phobia

Features: Irrational fears of certain objects or situations such as injections, the dentist, school, insects, thunderstorms or darkness.

The White Queen in Lewis Carroll's *Through The Looking Glass* explains what anticipatory anxiety is all about when she screams hysterically, expecting at any second to prick her finger. Her brooch finally slips and she stabs herself, recovering immediately. She smiles at Alice and remarks: "That accounts for the bleeding you see. Now do you understand the way things happen here?" Alice asks: "But why don't you scream now?" The White Queen replies: "Why, I've done all the screaming already."

The point is that in real life, anticipation may actually be far worse than exposure to say a spider or air travel.

Emphasizing the need to identify the true nature of specific phobia, writer Alice Neville complains that the term "school phobic is tossed around too lightly."[12] A fear of bullies or of making a silly mistake at school does not reflect a school phobia, she says. The real school phobic, she explains, cannot explain exactly what it is they are afraid of.

Prevalence: Lifetime prevalence is about 7 per cent for men and 16 per cent for women.[13]

Related disorders: Studies suggest that 50–80 per cent of people with a specific phobia may have an additional anxiety or mood disorder.

Diagnosis: Pointers include avoiding the feared object even if this may have far-reaching consequences. For example, someone's promotion might be dependent on flying but if they had a phobia of flying they may refuse.

Treatment options: These include systematic desensitization: the patient may be asked to relax, and then imagine their phobia, working from the least fearful to the most fearful components. Graded real-life exposure may follow. Anti-anxiety and antidepressant drugs may also be used.

Agoraphobia (specific phobia)

Agoraphobia is anxiety about being in places or situations from which escape may be embarrassing or difficult: for example, in a crowd or queue or on a bridge. If you suffer from a panic attack, you may be at risk of developing agoraphobia. Supposing, for example, you had your first panic attack in a supermarket queue. Living in fear of another attack, you may decide to avoid going into supermarkets – and then somewhere else. This shrinking world invariably has a profound effect on self-esteem and self-confidence. In turn this may lead to depression or heavy drinking (which is also associated with depression) and deteriorating relationships with family and friends. The best response is to see the onset of agoraphobia or panic attacks or any other kind of anxiety disorder as a warning sign that something is wrong with your life. Try re-evaluating it, ideally with help either from your doctor or a self-help group or both (see Resources).

Social phobia

Features: Persistent, chronic fear of being watched and judged by others. Social phobia can be severely disabling: it can interfere with routine activities and preclude speaking or performing in public. Often the onset of social phobia occurs around adolescence, so a lifelong social phobia could even stem from an embarrassing situation at school.

Prevalence: About 11 per cent of men and 15 per cent of women experience social phobia.[14] Although it usually starts during adolescence, often after a humiliating or embarrassing experience, it can begin later (as in Scott's case, see page 45). For example, social phobia may emerge for the first time in an individual promoted to a job involving public speaking.

Related disorders: Social phobia often occurs along with generalized anxiety disorders, specific phobias and panic disorder. A public speaking engagement, for example, may trigger a panic attack.

Diagnosis: Shyness, stage fright and performance anxiety is common, whereas social phobia produces clinically significant distress. In children, symptoms should last for more than six months before a positive diagnosis is made.

Treatment options: Psychological treatments are the best means of obtaining lasting relief. Drugs (including beta blockers, see page 68) may relieve performance anxiety. The *World Health Organisation Guide to Mental and Neurological Health in Primary Care* cites research suggesting that many patients (with social phobia and other phobias) will need no medication if they face their fears systematically.[15] Antidepressants may be needed if "graded exposure" treatment does not work or if the patient refuses it.

Post-traumatic stress disorder (PTSD)

Features: Reaction in the form of extreme stress to an event such as a car accident or major disaster involving death or threat of death or serious injury to the individual or others. This may include flashbacks, nightmares and intrusive memories. The sufferer avoids thoughts which remind them of the event and may become emotionally numb and detached. They may have difficulty staying awake or sleeping, or concentrating and they may be prone to angry outbursts and irritability.

Treatment options: Facing the trauma – hard though this may be – is often effective. Antidepressants may help if depression is prominent. Starting CBT about one month after the trauma has been recommended.

Scott's story

It all started five years ago when I was 22, and in a meeting with lots of other people. There was nothing special about it, but suddenly I was hit from nowhere – totally out of the blue. I now know that this was a panic attack. I became very rigid and nervous. I don't really get panic attacks any more, but I'm very nervous about people watching me.

This is what social phobia is all about. You're constantly thinking that people are watching you and monitoring you and it makes you even worse. I've more or less got myself into a habit where I am nearly always nervous, either at work or socially. The sweaty palms, the trembling hands, inability to look someone in the eye totally destroy your confidence and you drop right down to the bottom and have to build it up again. This is what I'm trying to battle against.

If there were a tablet or pill that would cure it, I'd take it. I've tried herbal remedies and other over-the-counter remedies. I haven't been to my GP because I don't think he'd understand or he'd think I was depressed or give me a tranquillizer. I'd rather overcome it by my own means.

The only person (apart from the people at Don't Panic*) who knows about my social phobia is my fiancée. I don't want people to think I'm a crazy man. I wouldn't want to tell my mum and dad because I'd hate them to think of me any differently – the same with my friends. I've been going out with my partner for seven years and I only told her this year – and that took a lot even though we were both quite drunk and it came out in an argument. It's been good to share it with her.

*see Further Information

Scott, 27, salesman

4 Healthy human to anxious person

"Worry is interest paid on trouble before it falls due."

American proverb

Healthy brain response vs anxiety disorder

Dan and Jack (fictitious characters) have both made the same mistake, forgetting to bring some vital papers to work. Dan interprets his forgetfulness as another bad omen for his career prospects. He has always been a worrier and is prone to panic. Jack, on the other hand, immediately arranges to have the papers picked up and actually buys more time, persuading his boss to delay the meeting to discuss them. If they were real people and you could look inside their brains, you would probably see entirely different patterns of neural activity. Let's go to a small nugget of tissue deep inside the limbic system (see opposite) called the amygdala. This is a repository of emotions, sensations, feelings and memory – including the primal memories of powerlessness and helplessness of infancy, early childhood and perhaps even life in the womb. The amygdala responds to stress hormones by registering fear. If it is exposed to high concentrations of stress hormones passing across the placenta of a worried mother, it may be sensitized to the stimulus of fear before birth.

It may subsequently react to stress by calling up frightening memories from the past, without evaluating the real scale of any particular threat. Dan's forgotten papers may not be that significant in the overall scheme of things, but the amygdala may react as if his very life depends upon them – triggering a "fight or flight" stress response.

While Dan became intensely worried by his forgetfulness, Jack focused his attention on resolving the problem. This is a critical difference, as engaging in non-emotional mental tasks inhibits the negative flow of emotions from the amygdala to the rest of the brain. This is why keeping busy is often said to be the source of happiness. It may also help to keep anxiety-provoking situations in check.

What happens in the brain to trigger a phobia?

Phobias can attach to any object – leaves, chicken legs, paperclips. But most phobias relate to certain types of things such as snakes, heights, sharp objects or large spiders. The human brain seems to be primed, to be fearful of these things: the knowledge that they are potentially dangerous is written into our genes.

Most people don't become phobic about these things though, because in today's world they do not usually constitute a threat. The latent terror has to be triggered by something that happens to the individual. Research has shown that a baby monkey will not at first be scared of a snake. But if it sees its mother reacting to one with alarm, it will forever after be scared of

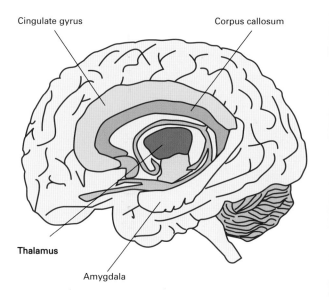

Cingulate gyrus

Corpus callosum

Thalamus

Amygdala

Emotions are generated within the limbic system – a cluster of organs in the centre of the brain, beneath the wrinkled grey cortex (see also diagram on page 50). Feelings of fear, sadness and rage originate in the amygdala.

them. The same is probably true of humans. This is not just a matter of mimicry – if a baby sees its mother reacting with fear to a flower, for example, it will just be puzzled.

Phobias of other objects – the chicken legs – are probably due to a conditioned response, similar to the salivation of Pavlov's dogs at the sound of a bell, which they had learned to associate with food. If a child first meets an innocuous object when they are already frightened, the fear is likely to become linked with the object, even if it is actually harmless. This is because memories are stored in a web-like pattern: any two things experienced at the same time are likely to be associated in the future.

Above: The experiments which Pavlov carried out with dogs prove that a bell used to signal food is on its way can provoke the same response as the smell of the food itself. Fear and anxiety can be instilled through conditioning similarly.

The Brain's Limbic System

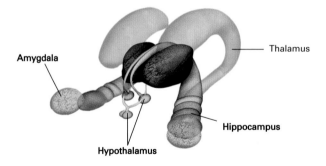

Amygdala

Thalamus

Hippocampus

Hypothalamus

Left: When the amygdala is strongly activated it creates a "knock-on" response in a neighbouring area, the hypothalamus. This, in turn, sends messages to the body to prepare for fight or flight.

How does the brain develop anxiety disorders?

The amygdala in the brain's limbic system generates negative emotions such as sadness, anger and fear, and it also stores bad memories. Engaging in non-emotional tasks can inhibit the negative flow of emotions from the amygdala. But if memory is "burnt" into the amygdala with enough force, it may be almost uncontainable and trigger such dramatic bodily reactions that a person may re-experience the precipitating trauma – complete with full sensory replay.

This condition, called post-traumatic stress disorder (PTSD), is quite clearly linked to a particular experience. PTSD was recognized in 1989 after American veterans who had returned from Vietnam suffered flashbacks and inability to sleep or concentrate. The diagnosis was later extended to cover survivors of rape, natural disaster, factory explosions and other terrors.

In 2003, Brian Engdahl, a psychologist at the Department of Veterans Affairs Medical Center in Minneapolis, in the USA, stated that a post-traumatic stress reaction had an adaptive value in evolution. He explained that the so-called "startle response" – an emotional and physiological reaction to an unexpected, sudden stimulus – has helped our species to survive. The startle response triggers a mechanism which "wires" the brain to remember the stimulus and to be on permanent alert against similar situations. [16]

PTSD, of course, is an extreme reaction. Sometimes the amygdala-based unconscious memories flood in without the corresponding conscious recollection that could pin them to a specific event. The irrational fear felt then may be vague – a thin cloud of anxiety – or it may be sudden and intense – a panic attack.

What drives obsessions?

The brain is driven by the need to keep the body alive and the in-built urge to reproduce. Everything else we do – from falling in love to making computers – is of secondary importance to the brain, a large portion of which is dedicated to pursuing food, sex and security. Sometimes the drivers of these urges break down, producing an inappropriate response which is repeated time and time again.

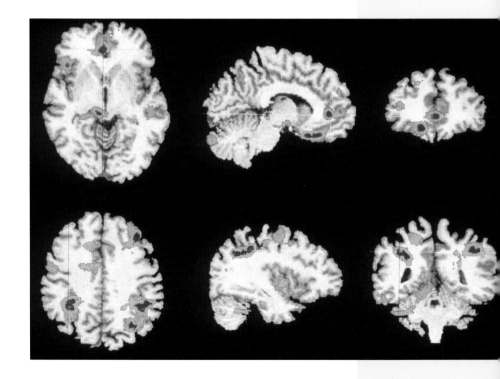

This is what happens in obsessive-compulsive disorder (OCD), the result of an overactive neural pathway between the frontal lobe of the brain and a part of the basal ganglia known as the caudate nucleus. The prompt we receive to wash when we are dirty or to check the front door is locked or that certain papers are in order comes from the caudate nucleus.

Ask a compulsive hand-washer to imagine themselves in some filthy place and the caudate nucleus and the orbital frontal areas of their brain will repeatedly fire and fire – setting off another round of ritualistic washing. You could only generate a similar response in a normal person by asking them to imagine a horrifying event such as their home going up in flames with the family unaccounted for. This person's brain would quickly revert to normal afterwards, but what about the compulsive hand-washer? The hand-washing compulsion may evaporate – but not for long. The circuit will soon glow again, rekindling the urge to wash. The error-detection mechanism has somehow become stuck on alert. No matter how often the appropriate switch-off action is applied, it continues to shriek out its warning.

In this PET scan (left) of a patient suffering from OCD, positive correlations (activity increasing as symptoms get stronger) can be seen in the top row, coloured in the left orbital region, prefrontal, left frontal gyri and thalamus. Negative correlation (activity decreasing as symptoms strengthen) is seen in the bottom row in the right frontal gyrus and parietal regions. Active areas coloured red or yellow show blood flow detected by a radioactive tracer. This highlights the role of the limbic system in its relationship with other areas of the brain.

Neurotransmitters

Neurotransmitters are chemical messengers which pass information between nerve cells or neurons – the basic units of the nervous system. Some neurotransmitters increase activity by stimulating cells to fire. Others decrease activity in certain parts of the brain. This transfer of information helps us to think, feel and act as different parts of the brain are activated. Four neurotransmitters known to be involved in anxiety and mood regulation are:

Gamma-aminobutyric acid (GABA) is the major inhibitory neurotransmitter of the central nervous system. Brain concentrations of GABA are reported to be 200–1000 times greater than the so-called monoamine transmitters such as serotonin, described opposite. GABA binds to neurons, blocking the transmission of electrical impulses, thus reducing communication between cells. Synthetic forms of GABA are used as tranquillizers, to damp down certain overactive circuits in the brain. This mimicking of the action of GABA can help in anxiety, but it also damps down almost every area of the brain, including those which produce anticipation, joy and desire.

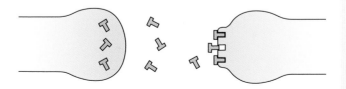

This illustration shows two neuron cells separated by a gap – the synapse. Millions of neurons form a communication system by transmitting impulses across the gap from neuron to neuron. These transmissions in turn signal to different parts of the brain and body.

Serotonin is known as the "feel good" chemical. Serotonin (5-hydroxytryptamine – 5HT) has a major effect on anxiety and mood. Drugs that increase its effect are the most common type of antidepressants. High serotonin concentrations are linked with optimism and serenity. As well as helping to regulate mood, it is involved in maintaining appetite, sleep and sexual activity and our response to the changing seasons. Fluoxetine (eg. Prozac) and similar drugs influence serotonin levels.

Noradrenaline (also known as norepinephrine) plays a key role in the body's response to acute stress and helps to maintain energy and mood. Found in the nerves that connect the brain with the heart and blood vessels, it stimulates the heart – priming the body for "fight or flight".

Dopamine helps promote feelings of happiness and well-being and is found in the areas of the brain which are associated with pleasure. Overly high levels of dopamine seem to be implicated in schizophrenia, a major psychiatric illness in which the different parts of the mind cease to function as an integrated whole, making the world a bewildering place where reality and fantasy may be indistinguishable.

5 Treatment options

"It is part of the cure to wish to be cured."

Seneca (4BC–65AD), Roman playwright and philosopher

Drug therapy

Drugs are regarded as a secondary rather than a primary treatment for anxiety disorders – as something to try if other measures don't work. For example, in the case of panic disorder, experts recommend initially turning to self-help groups, tapes, leaflets, breathing exercises, cutting down on caffeine, cognitive behaviour therapy (CBT) and not using cigarettes or alcohol as a prop. In one study of emergency treatment, researchers concluded that a few minutes of CBT advice improved patients' conditions on a long-term basis.[17] A professional guide for general practitioners advises that most patients benefit from the measures described above and need no medication unless their mood is very low.[18] The same guide advises that many phobic patients will need no medication if they face their fears systematically and that the outcome for patients with post-traumatic stress disorder "appears better after psychosocial approaches than after drug treatment".

Nonetheless, drug therapy has unquestionable benefits in some cases – sometimes even life saving. The selective serotonin re-uptake inhibitor (SSRI) family of antidepressants is now regarded as the first choice pharmacological treatment. (See page 60-61 for an explanation about why antidepressants are used to treat anxiety disorders.) Tranquillizers are now prescribed much less frequently because they are addictive if used for long periods. (See case history opposite.) Professor Peter Parish, author of a report called "The Prescribing of Psychotropic Drugs in General Practice" doubted claims they would "provide happiness when we are sad; energy when we are tired; sleep when we are wakeful; and clear thinking when our minds are 'cloudy'" which were over-optimistic. This is based on the argument that anxiety has a constructive role and that removing its sharp edges with medication can discourage people from taking stock of their problems, but most doctors have seen patients who have benefited from anti-anxiety drug therapy.

Julia's story

My experience of coming off tranquillizers was a nightmare. I went to see my GP, only to see a new doctor who told me I shouldn't be taking tranquillizers at all. He halved my prescription. I knew I was hooked, and that far from doing any good, the pills were doing me a lot of harm. I knew the doctor was 100 per cent right, but I felt very angry and dreadful – and very alone. My partner and I had been going through a very sticky patch and I couldn't talk to him. He just didn't understand. I have good friends, but I couldn't talk about this. The isolation is all part of the disease of addiction. You feel you are the only one with the problem

I read about Narcotics Anonymous and gave them a go. They were really helpful. It was such a relief to talk to people who knew exactly what I was talking about.

By this time I had already decided that I must stop the pills, and I was trying to wean myself off them. I had very severe withdrawal symptoms because I'd been taking them for about 20 years. When I finally stopped them altogether, it was absolute hell. I took five weeks off work and spent much of it in bed. I was so afraid, almost all the time, and convinced that I wouldn't make it. At one time I was hallucinating at 2am. But finally I did come out at the other end.

I felt as if I'd got out of prison and my brain started firing on all cylinders again. My memory is now much better. And since coming off the pills five years ago, I have never felt anxious or depressed.

Julia, 55, secretary

Antidepressants and anxiety disorders – the facts

Antidepressants act on neurotransmitters (monoamines such as serotonin) which play a key role in generating feelings of wellbeing. They seem to work by inhibiting or blocking the processes which lead to the destruction of monoamines or their removal from the synapse, the gap between adjoining nerve cells. This has given rise to the idea that depression is caused by low levels of monoamines. There is something in this idea, but it may not be the complete answer. Although neurotransmitter levels may be boosted within hours of someone taking an antidepressant, something else has to happen to lift the depression. Finding out what this is could be a major step towards better scientific understanding of depression. Anxiety and depression occur together in more than 50 per cent of cases.[19] Nearly two thirds of patients (62 per cent) with generalized anxiety disorder (GAD) also suffer from depression. Secondly, antidepressants have been found to be effective in treating anxiety-related symptoms such as tension, irritability and worry.

The pros: Studies have found that at least half of patients are much improved after three months of antidepressant treatment. The benefits can be dramatic and life transforming.

The cons: Benefits may be not sustained. While clinical trials suggest that up to half of patients with depression benefit, the figure is much lower in everyday clinical practice where treatment may not be supervised to the same extent. According to one report, as few as one in five patients (20 per cent) recover and subsequently maintain improvement for 18 months after drug therapy.[20]

Why are antidepressants used to treat anxiety disorders?

This is a book about clinical anxiety – the most common kind of mental health disorder. But anxiety and depression frequently occur together, with depression often following a period of anxiety. As the table below shows, out of every 1000 men and women in one survey, 44 were found to have generalized anxiety disorder (GAD). But 68 were reported to have "mixed anxiety and depression" – more than four times as many as those with phobias.

It is estimated that between 10 and 20 per cent of adults visit their doctor each year with an anxiety or depressive disorder. More than half of

This table shows the prevalence of mental disorders in men and women. The numbers shown are per 1000 men and 1000 women.

	Men	Women	Average
All neuroses	135	194	164
Mixed anxiety and depression	68	108	88
Generalized anxiety	43	46	44
Depression	23	28	26
Phobias	13	22	18
Obsessive-compulsive disorder	9	13	11
Panic	7	7	7
Personality disorder	54	34	44

Singleton N., Bumpstead R., O'Brien M. et al. *Psychiatric Morbidity Among Adults Living in Private Households*, Office of National Statistics, The Stationery Office, 2001

these are reported to have both clinical depression and anxiety and are at greater risk than patients with just one or the other. They are more likely to have a chronic condition, to take longer to recover and to have a recurrence. Research has shown that early effective drug therapy can reduce the risk of a long-term problem developing.

But how does a doctor determine if a patient is suffering from anxiety or depression or a combination of the two? Unfortunately, precise diagnosis is not always possible in mental disorders. This has led to the controversial suggestion that the medical distinction between anxiety and depression should be scrapped – a proposal that generated a hostile reaction in the letters column of the *British Medical Journal* in 2003.

Although named antidepressants, this group of drugs have many different pharmacological properties – some of which help anxiety disorders. The discovery of the first antidepressants highlights the diverse properties of antidepressants. Iproniazid, the very first, was initially developed in the 1950s to treat tuberculosis (TB). Doctors found that while it didn't improve TB, it did have a marked mood elevating effect. The second antidepressant, imipramine, was initially studied as a treatment for schizophrenia.

Why do antidepressants fail?

■ **Inappropriate prescribing:** Antidepressants are designed to treat people with moderate or severe problems. However, they are often prescribed for people with mild problems, sometimes because of lack of appropriate psychological therapies such as CBT.

■ **Side effects:** These may occur within a short time of starting treatment – before any therapeutic benefit emerges. Unaware of this mismatch between the onset of side effects and benefits, some patients stop treatment. Most side effects don't last long, but some do persist.

■ **Not knowing how long it takes for an antidepressant to work:** It may take several weeks for an antidepressant to achieve maximum benefit. Some patients give up treatment before the benefits are noticeable as they do not believe the medicine to be working.

■ **Giving up treatment when symptoms disappear:** Drug treatment should only be started and stopped in consultation with a GP.

■ **Forgetting to take medication:** This is a common problem, keeping a diary may help.

■ **Taking doses at the wrong time:** Two out of five patients are reported not to take drugs as instructed.

■ **The genetic factor:** There are wide variations in our responses to drugs.

■ **DIY experimentation:** Lowering or upping the dose without seeking medical advice first. Increasing the dose will not necessarily enhance the therapeutic effect and lowering it will not necessarily stop any unwanted side effects.

■ **A dose that is too high or too low:** Effective prescribing means finding the right balance between a dose that is high enough to work and low enough to prevent side effects.

How do benzodiazepine tranquillizers work and what are their risks and benefits?

Benzodiazepine tranquillizers increase the effects of a natural brain chemical called gamma-aminobutyric acid (GABA). GABA is a neurotransmitter – and a natural tranquillizer. It slows down activity within the brain by blocking the transmission of electrical impulses, reducing the output of neurotransmitters which play a key role in memory, emotional responses and alertness. According to one theory, the brains of people with anxiety disorders might race or work too fast because of malfunctioning GABA. The benzodiazepines are fast acting, having an almost immediate effect. They are only prescribed for short term (2–4 weeks maximum) or emergency use in treatment of generalized anxiety disorder, panic disorder and social phobia. In contrast, antidepressants, which are also used to treat anxiety disorders, may take several weeks to achieve their full effect. Individual response is variable. It is easy to see why with these apparent benefits, they became popular and relied upon, though they are associated with serious risks which should be considered before use.

The biggest problem is addiction related to prolonged use. (See page 66 for warning signs of potential dependence.) Other problems may include:

- Over-sedation, which may cause poor concentration, dizziness, mental confusion, muscle weakness and affect co-ordination.

- Loss of memory about recent events.

- Anxiety, insomnia and other so-called "paradoxical effects", including aggressive outbursts. Occasional cases of violent behaviour indicative of extreme aggression have been attributed to benzodiazepines.

■ Depression. This may be associated with the reduction in the output of neurotransmitters such as serotonin and noradrenaline, which help to regulate feelings of wellbeing.

■ Inhibition of functions regulating adjustment. It has been suggested that this may affect the ability to adjust to new stress management approaches, including cognitive behaviour therapy. A recent study has challenged the idea that benzodiazepines also inhibit the natural grieving process.

The Resources section contains details of self-help groups who offer advice and support about tranquillizer addiction. Many studies have concluded that 50 to 100 per cent of long-term tranquillizer users experience withdrawal symptoms which make it hard to stop taking the pills. About two per cent of the US population (four million people) were reported in 1990 to have used benzodiazepines for five to ten years or more. The situation is reported to be similar in most European countries.

The chart on page 67 lists withdrawal symptoms linked with reducing or stopping tranquillizers. Any symptoms experienced while taking tranquillizers can be withdrawal symptoms if they become a great deal worse and different after stopping them. Some patients blame any new symptoms on withdrawal – which can delay the diagnosis of any serious new condition.

Here again it is important to establish which symptoms are linked to withdrawal. Knowing your symptoms may help the doctor to tailor the rate of withdrawal to your individual needs, taking into account factors such as lifestyle, personality and support. It is generally agreed that dosage should be tapered gradually in long-term benzodiazepine users.

Warning signs of potential tranquillizer dependence

People who become addicted to medically prescribed benzodiazepines may show several of these features: [21]

■ They continue to take the medication even though the original reason for doing so no longer exists.

■ They rely on tranquillizers to undertake daily routine activities like work, shopping, running the home, mixing with people and travelling.

■ They have taken medication in prescribed "therapeutic" doses for months or years. (Psychological or physical dependence may develop within a few weeks or months of regular use.)

■ They cannot stop their medication because of withdrawal symptoms. Addicts often believe they may not be able to manage at all without tranquillizers and in some cases believe that they will always need to take the drugs.

■ They may have increased the dose of the first prescription.

■ They may have symptoms of anxiety, depression, panic attacks, agoraphobia and insomnia.

■ They may take an additional dose to cope with a stressful event.

■ They crave their next dose.

Withdrawal symptoms after stopping tranquillizers

Mild withdrawal symptoms:	Severe withdrawal symptoms:	Unlikely withdrawal symptoms:
■ muscle tension	■ severe depression	■ tinnitus
■ sweating	■ muscle twitching	■ vomiting
■ trembling	■ burning sensations	■ thought control
■ dizziness	in the skin	■ missing heart
■ headaches	■ hallucinations	beats
■ nausea	■ paranoid symptoms	■ loss of hair
■ loss of appetite	■ confusion and	■ obesity
■ blurred vision	memory loss	■ allergy to foods
■ phobias	■ delusions	■ skin rashes [22]
■ increased sensitivity	■ epileptic fits	
to noise and light	■ impressions of	
■ weakness in arms	objects moving	
and legs	when still	
■ panic	■ unreality	
■ tingling in hands	(depersonalization	
and feet	and derealization)	
■ loss of interest	■ severe joint pains	
■ inability to	■ incontinence of	
concentrate	urine	

Abrupt withdrawal, especially from high doses, can trigger severe symptoms. Even with slow withdrawal from smaller doses, psychiatric symptoms sometimes appear and anxiety can be severe. See your doctor if any symptoms persist – including the mild ones – and if you develop any of the severe symptoms in column two.

This table is adapted from How to Stop Taking Tranquillizers *by Dr Peter Tyrer (Sheldon Press, 1986). The "mild withdrawal symptoms" listed in the first column are very common in states of anxiety and may not necessarily be linked to tranquillizer withdrawal. The symptoms in the final column (unlikely symptoms) are most unlikely to be related to tranquillizer withdrawal, but may be wrongly attributed to it. They should be investigated to establish their real cause.*

Other drugs for treating anxiety disorders

Beta blockers: These inhibit the "fight or flight" reaction which primes the body for rapid action, dampening down physical symptoms of anxiety disorders, such as a rapid heartbeat, fast breathing, hand tremors and sweating. Beta blockers are also used to treat angina and high blood pressure and probably have no direct effect on emotions such as worry and fear. Relieving *physical* symptoms can ease psychological ones.

Antihistamines: Used to treat allergies, antihistamines can have a relaxing effect and may help severe anxiety symptoms.

Major tranquillizers or antipsychotics: People with psychoses lose touch with reality and are at risk from disorders such as schizophrenia. These illnesses are totally different to anxiety disorders, but some major tranquillizers can have a calming effect. They work by reducing the effects of dopamine, a neurotransmitter that helps control emotions, thoughts and movements. Major tranquillizers are not a "first line" treatment for anxiety disorders but may be used if other treatments fail or if symptoms intensify.

Hand tremors, along with other physical symptoms that are an outward sign of nervousness, are reduced by the action of beta blockers.

Buspirone: This is regarded as an attractive alternative to the benzodiazepines because it is not addictive – you can stop taking it without experiencing withdrawal symptoms. It is not generally seen as a first line treatment because it takes two to three weeks to start working. The American psychiatrist David D. Burns, author of *The Feeling Good Handbook*, comments: "It is thought to be only somewhat effective for generalized anxiety and social phobia and less effective for other forms of anxiety such as panic attacks or obsessive-compulsive disorder." [23]

Complementary medicine

More than 40 per cent of people suffering anxiety attacks had tried complementary medicine in the previous year, says a recently published report. [24] This demonstrates the phenomenal demand for complementary medicine in Europe and the USA. This patient-driven, medical, counter culture has been interpreted as a response to the technical failure of disease-orientated modern medicines to live up to their own promise in terms of curing illness and enhancing quality of life; and to concern about the side effects of pharmaceutical drugs – especially tranquillizers.

The Desktop Guide to Complementary and Alternative Medicine [25] by Professor Edzard Ernst describes 14 different therapies for anxiety disorders which can be used as "stand alone" treatments or in combination with other approaches. The new "pick 'n' mix" medical culture is forging a growing partnership between complementary and scientific medicine. For example, simple breathing exercises or yoga or relaxation training are now often recommended as a supplement to drug therapy.

A common criticism of complementary medicine is that it is not tested scientifically, as conventional treatment has to be. The therapies in the chart on page 70, however, have been scientifically evaluated – to a greater or lesser extent. The chart highlights the most successful therapies and the scientific evidence in favour of each. The method by which Ernst determined "weight of evidence" based on several factors has been included.

Science cannot measure the success of everything, and what it does measure reflects what is best for the majority. No one medical treatment has every answer to every medical problem.

Check the qualifications of any complementary practitioner before consulting them. Establish if they are affiliated to a professional body or register. See Resources for organizations that can provide a starting point.

Treatment	Weight of evidence	Direction of evidence	Serious safety concerns
Aromatherapy	••	↗	Yes
Autogenic training (AT)	••	↗	Yes
Biofeedback	••	→	No
Electro-stimulation	••	↗	Yes
Exercise	•	↑	Yes
Homeopathy	•	→	No
Hypnotherapy	•	↗	Yes
Massage	•	↗	No
Meditation	••	↑	Yes
Music therapy	•	→	No
Relaxation	•••	↑	No
Spinal manipulation Chiropractic	•	↓	Yes
Spiritual healing	•	↑	No

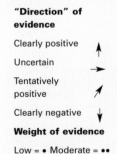

"Direction" of evidence

Clearly positive ↑

Uncertain →

Tentatively positive ↗

Clearly negative ↓

Weight of evidence

Low = • Moderate = ••
High = •••

The weight of evidence refers to the importance that can be placed on it determined by three factors: 1) the level of evidence, 2) the quality of the investigation and 3) the volume of information (number of studies). The direction of evidence refers to the collective outcome, positive or negative of the trials that were used in Ernst's study.

Clinical study of complementary therapies

Complementary therapies are often thought of as "safe" because they are natural – this is not true. Natural products can be just as harmful as manufactured products if used incorrectly. For example, the essential oils used in aromatherapy should not be taken by mouth or used undiluted on the skin. Some oils cause photosensitive reactions, some have carcinogenic (cancer-causing) potential, and some may cause allergic reactions, nausea and headache. Many essential oils are believed to have the potential to enhance or reduce the effects of prescription medicines, including tranquillizers. Check the potential risks of any complementary therapy before starting it. The following list summarizes the most commonly available complementary therapies that have been proven effective in anxiety disorders. The summaries of research findings in this section and the table to the left have been adapted from *The Desktop Guide to Complementary and Alternative Medicine (CAM),* edited by Professor Edzard Ernst, which presents a comprehensive review of the scientific evidence about the effectiveness of complementary therapy.

Aromatherapy

What is it?: Treatment with highly concentrated oils extracted from plants. Known as essences or essential oils, these highly scented extracts contain the substances that give plants their smell. Essential oils activate the olfactory (smell) sense, triggering the limbic system, the part of the brain governing emotional responses. Hundreds of plants produce essential oils, but most aromatherapists use about 30 for most conditions.
Treatment: Oils can be applied directly to the skin via a massage or a

compress; added to a bath; inhaled with steaming water or spread throughout a room with a "diffuser" such as a candle. You can either see an aromatherapist or try a DIY treatment. (See Further Information, page 165.) A massage by an aromatherapist can have a calming effect.

What the research says: There are clearly significant effects, but these are short-term and probably too modest to be clinically relevant. Aromatherapy does appear to be a beneficial palliative or supportive treatment.

Autogenic training (AT)

What is it? A series of six mental exercises which is reported to turn off the "fight or flight" stress response and induce a state of calm similar to that of meditation.

Treatment: All six exercises can be carried out in any one of three positions – the reclining position; the armchair position; or the simple sitting position. Each exercise directs thought to a particular sensation or part of the body. For example, "heaviness exercises" focus on heaviness in the arms, legs and shoulders; while "breathing exercises" cultivate awareness of breathing. Each exercise involves silently repeating a phrase such as: "My right arm is heavy." This can produce feelings of warmth and heaviness and a slowed heartbeat.

What the research says: Although poor quality research prevented firm conclusions, the overall outcome was positive, but the use of AT did not show a significant reduction in panic attacks.

Biofeedback

What is it? Self-monitoring with electronic apparatus of physiological responses such as heart rate, blood pressure, muscle tension, provides information to help people gain greater control over mind and body. Traditional Eastern practices such as yoga have similar aims.

Treatment: The patient is wired up to the monitoring equipment and various physiological responses (such as those above) are monitored. They are then converted into audio or visual signals. Any change in physiological function is marked by a change in the audio or visual signal. The ultimate idea is to learn how to recognize significant physiological changes without any help from electronic equipment.

What the research says: Biofeedback has been shown to be successful. Reviews suggest that combining relaxation therapy with biofeedback is an effective treatment – more so than relaxation therapy alone. (See page 76).

Homeopathy

What is it? Based on the principle that "like cures like", homeopathy is known as "the magic of the minimum dose". It uses minute amounts of diluted substances derived from plant, animal and mineral extracts. The doses are uniquely small – so small that they lack pharmacologically active molecules.

Treatment: The homeopath seeks to understand the action and interaction of many different factors which might affect and cause a disease. For example, they may ask if the patient prefers hot or cold weather, the sea or mountains, whether he is quick-tempered or sulky. They then "match" physical and mental characteristics to determine the appropriate remedy.

What the research says: On current evidence, the value of homeopathy cannot be confirmed or denied. There is no scientific rationale for assuming that such remedies work.

Kava

What is it? A herbal ingredient derived from a plant which belongs to the pepper family native to many Pacific Ocean islands, it contains relaxation-inducing chemicals called lactones. Research suggests that Kava may have a similar calming effect to tranquillizers, increasing the effect of gama-aminobutyric acid (GABA), a brain chemical which slows down brain activity.

Treatment: The ingredient is often added to liquid and taken internally.

What the research says: In recent years Kava has become popular throughout Europe in herbal remedies for treating anxiety, tension and restlessness. In a review of seven studies, it was shown to be better in treating anxiety than a placebo or dummy treatment. But the sale of Kava was banned in the UK in 2003 after 70 reports worldwide of suspected adverse reactions. These include four cases of fatal liver toxicity and seven cases in which patients required liver transplants.

Hypnotherapy/hypnosis

What is it? A trance-like state, known as the Alpha state, which makes people more susceptible to suggestion, enabling them to increase control over their thoughts and feelings.

Treatment: It may involve 6–12 weekly sessions, each between 30 and 90 minutes. The alpha state has been compared to the time when we wake up in the morning and cannot quite open our eyes, even though we are aware of sounds outside the house or a distant radio. We either can't or don't want to wake up and open our eyes.

What the research says: Hypnosis is used extensively to treat dental phobia, but it has been found to be no more effective than group therapy and "desensitization" – encouraging patients to overcome their fear by slowly exposing them to it – for example, by having a simple scale and polish rather than more invasive treatment. Hypnosis has also been shown to be an effective way of relieving anxiety among children before stressful medical procedures like lumbar puncture.

Massage

What is it? Probably the oldest therapy known to man, massage is a means of manipulating soft tissue with pressure. Touch is an important means of conveying a sense of caring and of locating muscle tension. In some European countries, including Germany, massage is part of conventional medicine.

Treatment: A typical session lasts about 30 minutes. The patient is normally undressed, with a towel provided. The main forms of massage include effleurage (slow rhythmic strokes); percussion or tapotement (short fast rhythmic drum-like movements, usually performed with the side of the hands on the back or a fleshy part of the body); pétrissage (grasping and squeezing sections of muscles) and friction (a series of small circular movements by one or more fingers).

What the research says: Research highlights positive benefits. For example, in one study with depressed pregnant adolescents, the group receiving massage therapy for five weeks fared better than the group having relaxation therapy. Anxiety levels in both groups fell, but the massage group also slept better, had less back pain and their mood lifted.

Meditation

What is it? In normal consciousness the mind flits from subject to subject. In meditation it focuses upon a single image or idea. The aim is to narrow down the focus of attention to a state where ordinary awareness transcends to a more intense plane of consciousness. Meditation has profound physiological as well as psychological repercussions, which promote relaxation and calm. Oxygen consumption can fall by as much as 16 per cent within minutes, heart rate can fall by as much as a third, the respiratory rate may be halved.

Treatment: This takes the form of learning meditation techniques.

What the research says: Meditation has proven benefits in reducing anxiety levels.[26]

Relaxation therapy

What is it? There are many different kinds of relaxation therapy, including visualization and breathing exercises (see opposite). You don't need a prescription for this kind of mind–body medicine. The Further Information section includes advice about where to go for additional advice.

What the research says: Relaxation therapy was found to be less effective than cognitive behaviour therapy (CBT) in treating panic disorder and as effective as CBT and exposure in treating agoraphobia. Exposure therapy involves gradually exposing the individual to their fear, usually under supervision. In one trial, patients with chronic obstructive airway disease were treated either with relaxation therapy or standard management alone.[27] The relaxation group fared better, with reduced anxiety and breathing problems. Audiotapes with relaxation instructions have been found to be more effective than music tapes in reducing anxiety and pain.

Summarizing the advice in the *Desktop Guide to Complementary and Alternative Medicine*, Ernst says: "Conventional psychological interventions are as successful as medications for anxiety and often more acceptable. For patients who are willing to undertake a mind–body approach, meditation, and to a lesser extent autogenic training or relaxation, can be encouraged. Electro-stimulation may also be recommended where it is available.* Relaxation is also useful for anxiety associated with particular conditions and medical procedures, although hypnotherapy appears more appropriate for children."

* Electro-stimulation involves mild battery-powered stimulation, usually through clip-on electrodes that are attached to the earlobes or by electrodes placed behind the ears. The flow produces a brief tingling sensation which is reported to leave the user alert and relaxed.

Exercise using visualization

You can use visualization in any one of a number of ways for specific therapeutic purposes. It is based on the principle that mind and body are intimately connected and that what changes one has an instant effect on the other. Visualization is also an extension of what we all do on a daily basis. When you cook a meal, you visualize the way you want it to look. You create what you imagine. So it is with therapeutic visualization. You can use it, for example, to help you confront a problem by imagining it. Imagine a job interview or a tough presentation, and how you are going to calm your nerves and promote positive thinking.

■ Sit comfortably.

■ Imagine the presentation, interview or other situation you dread is just starting. Accept your anxiety as normal, even helpful. It makes you feel alert, even excited.

■ Now visualize yourself during the presentation. How are you dressed? How does the room look? How do the other people look? (Of course, you don't know that – but however they look, is there any real reason why they should intimidate you?)

■ Visualize yourself as being calm and in control. The presentation is a great success. Repeat the procedure several times. Many successful sportsmen use visualization to spur themselves on to greater success.

Breathing

Breathing is a key physiological activity which responds to mental states. When we are under stress, our breathing becomes shallow. Breathing only to and from the top of the lungs exacerbates anger. Breathing exercises can have a calming effect and be used at any time (see also Resources).

6 Lifestyle

"...Nor, are we to give attention solely to the body; much greater care is due to the mind and soul; for they too, like lamps, grow dim with time, unless we keep them supplied with oil."

Cicero (106–43 BC), Roman philosopher, *De Senectute*, 45 BC

Anxiety and life-threatening illnesses like heart disease

An important question is, whether there is a link between emotional problems such as anxiety and life-threatening illnesses like heart disease? This book is mainly about problems of the mind, but mind and body function as one. Emotions affect our susceptibility to disease. For example, anxious and depressed people have been found to be at increased risk from a heart attack. Scientists have yet to establish why. One possibility is that anxiety can result in people adopting a less healthy lifestyle and becoming more reliant on "social crutches" like comfort food and alcohol.

This begs the question: what is a healthy lifestyle and what are the benefits? One of the most striking lifestyle studies of the last 50 years began in the typical Californian urban community of Alameda County in 1965. Long-term follow up of the 7000 people involved has shown a clear link between physical health on the one hand and longevity on the other – and what the researchers called "the seven health habits" (see opposite).

A 45-year-old man following six or seven of the habits was found to have a one-in-two chance of living to the age of 78; those following four or five habits of living to 73; zero to three habits of living to 67. There was a difference of 11 years life expectancy between the top and bottom groups. Among women the difference was four years less.

In every age group, people following seven habits had better physical health, on average, than those reporting six or less. The "physical health status" of the over-75s adopting seven good habits was similar to those aged 35–44 following less than three. Of course, good physical health will never confer immunity against anxiety, but it may reduce our susceptibility to stress-related disease – including heart attacks.

The seven health habits

In the study reported on the opposite page, the Human Population Laboratory included the following health-promoting habits.[28] Implementing these can help to reduce stress and anxiety as well as promoting physical health.

- **Never smoking cigarettes:** Smoking actually triggers a stress response. The sense of relaxation smokers feel when they smoke is caused by the relief of withdrawal or addictive symptoms.

- **Regular physical activity:** This has been shown to relieve anxiety symptoms as well as aid physical health. (See Endorphins: natural stress fighters on page 83).

- **Moderate or no use of alcohol:** Pharmacologically, alcohol is a central nervous system depressant. The apparently stimulating effect of drinking occurs when the alcohol inhibits or depresses the normal inhibitory processes in the brain.

- **Seven to eight hours sleep a day regularly:** Sleep not only provides us with physical rest, it is also a time when "psychological" sorting processes occur.

- **Maintaining proper weight:** Stress can make us fat as people often eat for comfort. Losing weight means either eating fewer calories or increasing your energy output through exercise.

- **Eating breakfast:** People in the California study who ate breakfast almost every day or did not eat between meals had slightly better health than those who skipped breakfast or ate between meals.

- **Not eating between meals**: Several small meals have been found to be better than one or two heavy ones, but constant snacking is to be avoided.

What are the psychological benefits of a physically active lifestyle?

Former radio presenter Ernest Dudley who ran the New York Marathon within only seven months of taking up running in his sixties put it this way: "You become aware that if you are physically fit, you think better. To be bodily virile means you are mentally alert. Your mind is activated to its fullest, and the power of your mind can be boundless: it can perform miracles. You earn for yourself an increased self-respect, your glowing health earns you a brighter self-image. With this increased physical fitness, this sense of wellbeing and mind-power, come self-confidence, a lesser need to rely on a drink to boost your morale, or another cigarette, or another helping from the food trolley to stiffen your resolve." [29]

This may make Dudley seem like an ageing Superman, but as a young man he had irrational phobic fears – they returned years later after the death of his wife when he again became convinced he had a life-threatening heart condition. He started running to "turn off" his fear – with phenomenal success.

This is not an isolated example of the liberating power of exercise. Many studies show that regular exercise makes people feel better – aiding relaxation, concentration and sleep. You may even feel less tired after exercise than before. (The following pages outline other possible options).

Exercise can also relieve anxiety and depression, according to many different studies. Just one session can produce at least a brief reduction in symptoms, while regular activity may have long-term beneficial effects. Running or walking also helps clarity of thought – which may explain the archetypal image of someone pacing up and down when they have a problem to think through. See page 84 for more on walking.

Endorphins: natural stress fighters

Physical exercise generates a cascade of biochemical activity in the brain – the basis of the feelings and emotions that Ernest Dudley describes with such passion on the opposite page. The brain produces neurotransmitters known as endorphins in response to a variety of stimuli – including exercise. These are believed to be nature's remedy for high stress levels. Pain is another stimulus which triggers the release of endorphins. These interact with the brain's opiate receptors to reduce our perception of pain – by blocking the release of neurotransmitters which carry pain "signals". We associate stress with pain, but as pointed out earlier, stress can also be exhilarating.

The secretion of endorphins can usher in a sense of euphoria and this is believed to explain the so-called "runner's high" that athletes experience with prolonged exercise. Blood levels of endorphins have been found to increase to as much as five times their resting levels during a prolonged bout of vigorous exercise.

Acupuncture and massage therapy, meditation and sex can also stimulate endorphin secretion – as can eating chocolate. This probably explains the comforting feeling that many people associate with chocolate in times of stress.

Walk don't run. Isn't walking actually better than running?

Thomas Jefferson (1743–1826), third US President, declared: "Of all exercises, walking is best." This may have been true for him; it may not be true for you – it is a matter of preference. You may prefer one of the options listed opposite. One major advantage of walking is that it requires no equipment or expense and can be built into your daily routine. Regular brisk walking can increase confidence, stamina, energy, fitness or weight loss and life expectancy and may reduce the risk of anxiety, stress and life-threatening conditions like heart disease and cancer.

You need only walk for 30 minutes, five days a week to get the health benefits. If it suits you to break this down into three sessions of 10 minutes walking per day, that's just as good. Walking one mile in 15 minutes is reported to burn about the same number of calories as running a mile in about 8.5 minutes.

Walking at an average of 4.1 miles per hour (only a third higher than the average walking speed of three miles per hour) has been found to be sufficient to raise the heart rate to a beneficial level. The idea is to make you breathe a little more heavily than usual and feel warmer, without leaving you hot, sweaty and out of breath.

James M. Rippe, former director of the Exercise Physiology Laboratory, University of Massachusetts Medical School, pointed out that walking was also an "excellent" way to lose weight. He explained: "The average 150-pound person burns approximately 100 calories walking a mile. People are often surprised to learn that if they take a brisk 45 minute-walk four times a week for a year, and don't increase the amount of food they eat, they will burn enough calories to lose 18 pounds." [30]

Exercise: your choice

	Stamina	Suppleness	Strength
Swimming	•••	•••	•••
Jogging	•••	•	••
Cycling	•••	•	•••
Aerobics	•••	•••	••
Football	••	••	••
Golf	•	•	••
Tennis	••	••	••
Brisk walking	••	•	•
Housework	•	•	••

The first priority is to choose something that you will enjoy. If you are not currently very active, try to do about 30 minutes of moderate-intensity physical activity at least five days a week. For example, brisk walking, energetic housework, gardening or swimming. You may want to try a combination – say, walking and swimming. Note that swimming is the only activity above with a three-star rating in every category.

•   = 1 star rating
•• = 2 star rating
••• = 3 star rating

Diet: what's the relationship between food and mood?

The major aim of dietary advice is to reduce the incidence of heart disease, cancer, stroke, diabetes and bowel problems. Similar advice can be offered for psychological functioning. For optimal mental functioning the following is recommended: [31]

- Eat regular meals. Small meals eaten regularly will keep you psychologically more efficient than one or two large meals a day.

- Eat breakfast: low blood sugar levels later in the morning adversely affect memory. Similarly, a mid-afternoon snack will help to keep you going when your energy levels begin to flag.

- You may need to decrease the amount of saturated fat and sugar in your diet and replace it with unrefined carbohydrates. Eat plenty of wholemeal bread, pasta and brown rice. Five or six portions of fruit and vegetables provide fibre, vitamins and minerals.

- Eat enough iron, especially if you are a woman. Liver and red meat offer excellent sources. Wholegrain cereals, pulses and green vegetables also offer iron, though it is less easily absorbed by the body. A Vitamin C drink like orange juice will aid iron absorption.

- Oily fish, such as herring, sardine, mackerel and salmon, comprise a good source of essential fatty acids, which play key roles in the brain. Pregnant and lactating women, in particular, should ensure that they have sufficient fatty acids because these are important for the developing brain of the foetus and child.

Keeping a food and mood diary

Diet may affect our mood, but it is just one of many factors that may do so, and it is unlikely to predominate. Many claims have been made about the wisdom of eating/not eating particular foods, but it is difficult to ascertain whether any alleged benefits are attributable to dietary change rather than a placebo effect. Merely believing in the power of a specific food to make you feel better/worse may have that effect.

Most of us can eat most foods in moderation without any significant ill effects, but in some people, certain foods are reported to exacerbate anxiety, panic attacks and other disorders. These include artificial additives, preservatives, chocolate, coffee, corn, eggs and milk products, oranges, soya, sugar, tomatoes, wheat products (such as bread, pasta and cakes) and yeast.

Keeping a food and mood diary for a week or more may help to establish any links between your symptoms and diet. The best way is to carry a small notebook around with you and to note down what you eat at the time and how much. You can also use pages 136–137 of this book to make notes of your food intake. The National Association for Mental Health (MIND) says: "The basis of a healthy diet is about achieving a balance between a wide variety of foods, where the variety – instead of being crammed into one day – is spread out over a number of days...It is often a combination of eating too much of some foods and not enough of others which may be contributing to symptoms such as depression or anxiety."

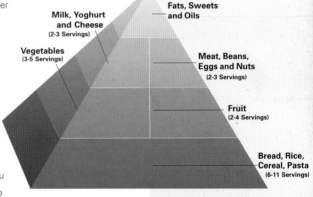

Fats, Sweets and Oils

Milk, Yoghurt and Cheese
(2-3 Servings)

Vegetables
(3-5 Servings)

Meat, Beans, Eggs and Nuts
(2-3 Servings)

Fruit
(2-4 Servings)

Bread, Rice, Cereal, Pasta
(6-11 Servings)

The food pyramid is an outline of what to eat each day for a balanced diet. It's not a rigid prescription, but a general guide that lets you choose a healthy diet that's right for you.

Part Two
Cognitive behaviour therapy

1 New ways of looking at thoughts and feelings

"Anxiety is a thin stream of fear trickling through the mind. If encouraged, it cuts a channel into which all other thoughts are drained."

Arthur Somers Roche, playwright

What is CBT?

Cognitive behaviour therapy (CBT) is all about the relationship between thoughts, feelings and behaviour. It is considered a new form of psychotherapy, but its philosophical foundations date back to the ancient Stoics of Greece, who applied a rational and logical approach to their understanding of man (and woman) and the senses. The philosophy of the Stoics has come to be known in the well-known adage "everything in moderation". Their philosophy was really an attempt to understand that we are products of our environment, and our emotions and feelings are physical processes. The philosophy behind CBT is perhaps best summed up by the Greek philosopher Epictetus in the 1st century AD. He observed: "People are disturbed not by things, but by the view they take of them."

William Shakespeare put it another way in *Hamlet*. In Hamlet's attempts to come to terms with the trauma of his father's death and his mother's betrayal with his uncle, he ponders: "There is nothing either good or bad, but thinking makes it so." It is easy to see how these statements apply in everyday life when one thinks of the many different ways there are of interpreting the things that happen to us. In fact everyone's experiences build up a unique perspective and set of feelings and thoughts, individual to them. For example, imagine yourself sitting in the airport lounge waiting to take off for the holiday of a lifetime. You may think: "I'm really looking forward to this." But if you are suffering from an anxiety disorder, built up over time, or as a result of a certain experience, you may become convinced that the plane is going to crash.

Inevitably, how you think affects how you feel – which in turn can affect how you behave. CBT offers a much simpler explanation of emotional problems than psychoanalysis, changing the way we think and what we do. In turn this affects how we feel.

The basis of CBT

CBT combines two very effective kinds of psychotherapy, cognitive therapy and behaviour therapy:

Cognitive therapy is based on the idea that changing thought processes can change behaviour ("cognitions" are thoughts). It was based on the original idea by the US psychiatrist Aaron Beck that some people develop mood disorders because (as a result of early learning experience) they develop negative thoughts and feelings about themselves. It is now used to treat a wide range of emotional disorders, including depression, anxiety disorders, eating disorders, shyness, substance abuse and addictive behaviour such as gambling. Cognitive therapy focuses on the power of mind and thoughts in shaping how we interpret the world and ourselves.

Behaviour therapy is based on the idea that changing behaviour will change thinking. It aims to break the links between stressful situations and negative habitual reactions to them. For example, a child bitten by a dog may develop a conditioned, fearful response to dogs as a result. The behaviourist may try to get them to relax in the presence of a dog or take them to a dog show to see dogs in the presence of dog lovers. The ultimate aim of therapy may be to persuade or condition the child to stroke a dog without fear and even to look forward to doing so – while realizing at the same time that some dogs are potentially dangerous. Once behaviour has changed – the child has stroked a dog without fear, for example – then new associations are made and the child's behaviour will subsequently be different around dogs.

The basic beliefs of behaviour therapy and cognitive therapy may seem diametrically opposed, but practising them in combination, as in CBT, derives the best from both approaches. CBT may sound as if it is a single type of therapy, but it encompasses a variety of different treatments. Some are predominantly cognitive in emphasis; some predominantly behavioural. The following are the primary practitioners and developers of CBT in the last century or so. If you follow the long chain of people back in time it takes you right to the birth of psychoanalysis.

Sigmund Freud (1856–1939). The father of psychoanalysis, Freud tried to explain the patient/client's condition by analyzing their past and subconscious. Modern critics say classical psychoanalysis focuses too much on the problem (and the *past*) and not enough on the solution (and the *future*). Freud, however, did understand that the past was intrinsically caught up in the present and future. "Neo-Freudians" have advocated a psychoanalysis that is more present and future orientated.

The Austrian psychologist, Sigmund Freud.

Ivan Petrovich Pavlov (1849–1936). The foundations for behaviour therapy were laid through Pavlov's famous set of behaviour-conditioning experiments with dogs, (see page 50). Our mouths (and those of the dogs in the experiment) water or salivate when we smell food. Pavlov's experiments showed that a bell signalling that food is on the way can prompt the same conditioned response, just through "association", i.e., if a bell is usually rung at dinner-time.

John B. Watson (1878–1958). The father of behaviourism, Watson was one of the leaders of a revolt against psychoanalysis and was heavily influenced by Pavlov. Watson switched the dominant force in psychology from thinking to learning – from the study of consciousness to observable behaviour.

Burrhus Frederick Skinner (1904–1990). Skinner developed "operant conditioning", which aims to relieve anxiety and fear by conditioning behaviour and rewarding change. For example, someone who is afraid of flying may be encouraged to go into a flight simulator and gradually, over time, overcome their fear. The aim is to make the visit a bearable experience.

Aaron Beck (1921–). Initially trained as a psychiatrist and a psycho-analyst, Beck became disenchanted with the Freudian approach and its emphasis on the unconscious. Beck believes that the answer to many emotional problems lies closer to the surface – and our conscious selves – than many Freudians would suggest.

Albert Ellis (1913–). Another pioneer of CBT, Ellis developed "rational emotive behaviour therapy", which aims to eliminate self-defeating beliefs through a rational examination of them.

The excerpt (right) demonstrates how far CBT has changed even since the last century, when behaviourists and classical psychoanalysts were at loggerheads.

"The psychoanalysts and the behaviourists showed little respect for one another. Both were convinced that they and they alone understood the secret springs of human motivation, according to the British psychiatrist, Robert E. Kendall. While psychoanalysis had been 'fatally wounded by its unscientific attitudes and the procedures and therapeutic impotence of its practitioners', Kendall maintained, behaviourism had been discredited by its 'association with brainwashing and failure to recognize the emotional and intellectual differences between a human patient and a rat'."

Foreword, *Cognitive Therapy for Depression and Anxiety*, Ivy Marie Blackburn and Kate Davidson, Blackwell Science, 1995

2 Understanding CBT

"Fears are educated into us and can, if we wish, be educated out."

Karl A. Menninger (1893–1990), US psychiatrist and author

What makes CBT work?

Imagine yourself doing a jigsaw. You have more or less completed the picture, but however hard you try, you cannot manage to slot in the last few pieces. You spend ages turning the pieces upside down and back hoping they will fall into place and reveal the true image; and yet the gaps just seem to get bigger. Just as you are about to give up, a friend or partner looks over your shoulder and says: "Are you sure that bit fits there?" You immediately realize you have forced a piece into the wrong place – you had no chance of finishing the puzzle and seeing the overall true picture.

In effect, this is what happens in anxiety disorders. People cannot see the overall true picture. All the little pieces of information, which your brain sorts and assimilates cannot be fitted together. There is something fundamentally wrong and the result is what Beck describes as an "over-active" alarm system: susceptible people are so aware of the possibility of harm that they constantly warn themselves about potential risks. Almost any stimulus may be enough to trigger the warning system and create "a false alarm". He observed: "The consequence of the blizzard of false alarms is that the patient does experience harm – he is in a constant state of anxiety." The anxiety becomes self-fulfilling.

This is where CBT can help. Using the jigsaw analogy, you may need to take the puzzle apart bit by bit before you can put it back together again. This means relearning and retraining your brain to assimilate information in a different way. There may be a vital ingredient (or piece of the puzzle) which you are missing, and by analyzing the way you think you may be able to get the missing piece. This may stop you falling into the "anxiety trap" (see page 100), in which negative feelings become self-perpetuating. Many theorists see people with emotional problems as victims who can exert little if any control over their feelings and it is easy to see why someone with a tendency to anxiety, can easily fall into the anxiety trap.

"In the anxiety state, the fear is so severe, persistent and pervasive that it colours every thought during every waking moment. There is an overwhelming sense of foreboding that something terrible is about to happen...As anxiety deepens, stress becomes more intense until the individual is reacting to almost everything in life. A slight noise will make him jump out of his skin, and in severe cases he is living with sheer terror. Not being able to define the problem makes the feeling of dread even worse."

The Complete Guide to Stress Management, **Chandra Patel, Optima, 1989**

What is the basic thinking underpinning CBT?

Although many different types of CBT are used to treat anxiety disorders, they all maintain that:

■ The way we interpret and assess information (think and feel) affects our behaviour.

■ Anxiety and depression promote negative thinking.

■ Identifying and changing negative thinking can relieve anxiety.

Beck isolated certain characteristics of anxiety disorders:

■ Repetitive thoughts about danger: the patient is preoccupied with a persistent irrational flow of thoughts about impending danger. These are the "false alarms" discussed opposite.

■ Reduced capacity to process the fearful thoughts: although the individual may know or suspect that they are behaving in an irrational way, they cannot weigh up or quell their anxiety-provoking thoughts.

■ Stimulus generalization: almost any sight or sound or change is perceived as a threat. For example, a woman hears an ambulance siren in the high street and is convinced her daughter is injured in an accident. Later she hears a car engine backfiring and believes a gunman is trying to murder her husband. (This is an extreme example.) Albert Ellis called this "catastrophizing" – the susceptible individual is gripped by the fear of the worst possible outcome in a particular scenario. While the anxiety of an average person decreases as they adjust to a stressful situation, the anxiety-prone individual is increasingly worried. In one study reported by Gelder and Marks in the *Journal of Psychosomatic Research* (1967; 11: 283–290), researchers exposed normal and highly anxious people to a collection of sounds. Both groups reacted by sweating, but while the normal group adjusted, the anxious group continued to sweat, suggesting that their anxiety was increasing. They were unable to discriminate between the "safe" and the "not safe". In fact, physical processes take over very quickly – which helps explain how panic attacks grip sufferers in moments (see below).

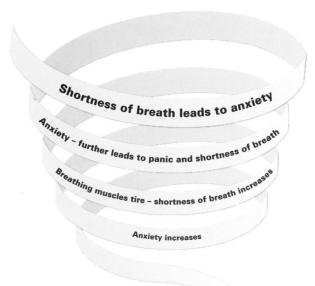

Shortness of breath leads to anxiety

Anxiety – further leads to panic and shortness of breath

Breathing muscles tire – shortness of breath increases

Anxiety increases

This diagram shows that, in panic attacks, mood disorder is manifested as significant physical symptoms.

So: people with anxiety disorders don't think straight?

That is one way of putting it. CBT therapists talk about logical errors in thinking. For example, an error may arise from failure to accurately assess the potential danger of a situation. Tony's business was doing well despite deteriorating trading conditions. Listening to a TV programme, he heard people in the same business complaining about declining sales. Rather than taking comfort in his own strong position and working out how to build on it, he suffered a severe crisis in confidence – observed by his customers.

Another common error in logical thinking results from people thinking about the negative not the positive. This is not to say that the philosophy of CBT is based on the power of positive thinking. Of course, positive thinking is important, but it probably won't work (or it won't work for very long) unless you first understand the root cause of your problem. If you paint over rust, the initial gloss may look smart – but it won't last. We will be looking at ways to address problems later on. Thinking negatively can mean assuming that a wart is cancer to fearing anything from a massive heart attack after an innocent flutter or palpitation.

Over-generalizing – reaching a general conclusion about a situation on the basis of one factor alone – is another common logical error in thinking. A typical case might see a highly successful young teacher with good communication skills and flair for the classroom perceiving themselves as a failure because they were unable to control one unruly pupil. Such a negative self-belief would have corrosive effect on confidence – demonstrating how blowing a problem out of all proportion results in a cognitive chain reaction.

The cognitive chain reaction

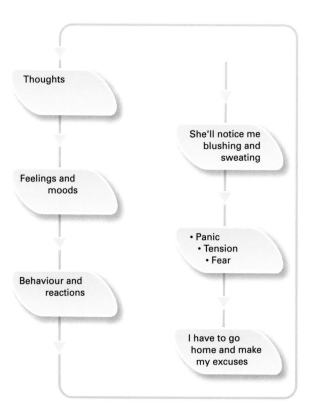

Thoughts

She'll notice me blushing and sweating

Feelings and moods

• Panic
• Tension
• Fear

Behaviour and reactions

I have to go home and make my excuses

A man with social phobia at a party becomes more and more self-conscious as he talks to a woman he has just met. He wants to cultivate her friendship but cannot control his phobia. He fears that he will be unable to sustain a conversation and seem silly or boring and takes refuge in heavy drinking – further distancing himself from her.

Is there some kind of mental mechanism that blocks logical thinking?

Yes. This produces so called "negative automatic thoughts" – mental reflexes that just pop into our heads without being in the forefront of our minds. We may *automatically* accept them even if they are distorted or irrational. They can have an all-embracing effect, influencing the way we see ourselves, the way we see the world around us and the way we see the future. (See page 99–100 for the different types of ways our brains can overreact.)

Any negative or dysfunctional thoughts and feelings we develop about ourselves are reflected in "schemata", the building blocks of cognition. These are the attitudes and assumptions that shape our beliefs about ourselves, other people and the world around us. In his book, *Vital Lies, Simple Truths: The Psychology of Self-Deception,* Daniel Goleman describes memory as "autobiography".[1] He explains: "Its author is 'the self', an especially potent organization of schemas. Sometimes also called 'the self system; or self concept', it is that set of schemas which define what we mean by 'I', 'me' and 'mine', that codify a sense of one's self and one's world."

Goleman is talking about what is better known as "self-image" or "self-esteem". Most of us know what we mean by self-esteem or self-image without necessarily having thought very much about where it comes from.

The origin of your schemata will date back to your childhood and the relationships you had with your parents, family and classmates – and other people who are prominent in your life. How do you interpret these relationships and what they say about you? How do you put together the mental building bricks which make up your schemata?

We usually regard our schemata as statements of fact. They produce core beliefs – which may be positive or negative. Once activated, a negative core belief can produce a cognitive shift away from the positive. What this means is that the susceptible individual begins to distort incoming information to fit into their negative schemata. The page opposite shows examples of positive and negative responses to the kinds of situations we all experience.

Goleman talks about "the self" as having in its power all the tools and temptations of a totalitarian state. The self, he says, acts like a censor, selecting and deleting information to make it compatible with the prevailing schemata.

The aim of CBT is to address this "censor" and to challenge any false assumptions and change an anxious self schema into a healthy one.

Schemata in anxiety disorders often relate to the need to be in control, or to stay calm, or to be able to avoid new situations. Research suggests that basic schemata lie dormant during periods of remission. They may be reactivated during times of stress by specific triggers. The "self censor" within the brain then applies them to an increasing number of situations, resulting in more and more distorted thinking.

The grid opposite shows how negative self-schemata manifest themselves in everyday situations.

Situation	Negative responses	Positive responses	Negative self-schema
You're preparing a speech for a business presentation at very short notice.	I'm going to mess this up. There's just not enough time to do the material justice.	I'm going to be as well prepared as possible. The tight deadline is focusing my mind on the key issues.	Lack of drive, self-doubt and lack of confidence.
You're going out with someone you like for the very first time.	I'm going to make a fool of myself and say all the wrong things.	It's great that she wants to see me. I must try and make the evening really good for both of us.	Lack of self-esteem, poor self-image, hiding away.
You're having a routine blood test.	This will confirm everything I've been dreading.	I don't think there's anything to worry about, but best be sure.	Self-obsession, self-absorbed.
Your friend is late turning up for a meeting.	He's been in a road accident.	This gives me the chance to catch up.	Self-doubt, self-blame, feeling powerless.

3 Approaches to treatment

"The cognitive approach brings the understanding and treatment of emotional disorders closer to a patient's everyday experiences."

Aaron T. Beck, *Cognitive Therapy and the Emotional Disorders*, Penguin Books, 1989

CBT today

In starting CBT, you may feel as if you are undergoing a culture shock. It involves forgetting the idea of being "a patient" and thinking of yourself more as part of the emotional health-care team. Collaboration is one of the key principles of CBT: you and the therapist will work together to resolve your anxiety problem. You may be asked to imagine yourself working as a scientist – and even treating your anxiety disorder as a scientific idea or hypothesis that must be tested. You will be expected to collect and evaluate data to test it. Just what is the basis of your irrational thoughts? Is there another way of looking at them?

This approach is in line with the new health-care model which recognizes the patient as "an expert" in their own right, and therapist and patient as a partnership. Being an "expert patient" is not a soft option, especially in CBT. Again, imagine yourself working as a scientist – this time, at home alone. This may involve, for example, keeping a diary or monitoring fluctuations in the way you feel on a chart. The overall process can be hard work and CBT is not for everyone, but it has been shown to work in a large number of cases.

In *Patients and their Doctors* (1979), consultant psychiatrist Glin Bennet, then of Bristol University, in the UK, observed: "The success of medical science has engendered a sense of passivity in the minds of the lay public which has flattered the doctor's sense of power and self-esteem. It has also caused people to assume less and less responsibility for what happens to their bodies and minds. The greatest benefit could come in the future if patients could take on more responsibility for their bodies and minds." [2]

Now, a quarter of a century later, CBT is reflecting a new and ever-growing belief in the power of health-care management systems designed with the new patient–doctor relationships in mind.

What CBT treatment involves

Time: Allow for up to 10 or more weekly sessions, each lasting up to an hour.

Aims and objectives: These are determined at the start of each session and may take 10 minutes or so. You will be asked what you want to talk about. This is an important part of setting the agenda and deciding targets. Time is allocated for specific talking points and targets are set.

Style: CBT is designed to promote an efficient, target-based approach, but there is no magic formula. Different approaches work for different people. Working out what's best may involve trial and error and breaking down anxiety-related problems into different components which can show problems in a new perspective.

Homework: This is a critically important part of any CBT programme. Assignments may include keeping an anxiety or panic diary and mood monitoring. Homework is routinely reviewed.

Feedback: The therapist may seek constant feedback to see how the client feels about the session. This also reduces any risk of the client not speaking out if the session makes them anxious or depressed. At the same time, when someone who tends to get overly anxious is asked the reasons for their anxiety, it can often help them realize their feelings are groundless. Sometimes they may begin to feel that they are not as anxious as their brain would lead them to believe. In general the complex effects of CBT make it difficult to trace the attainment of goals, but making and keeping to targets and constantly evaluating progress is undertaken by patient and therapist together.

What are the CBT treatment techniques?

A large range is used – some for treatment sessions, some for homework assignments, some for both.

Examining the evidence for and against a negative thought

Mary's case, outlined on page 21, highlights the basic treatment approach. She had her first panic attack shortly after her mother's death when she was having problems at school. She recalls: "I had just got off the bus and I felt something was terribly wrong, although I couldn't have told you what it was. Very shortly afterwards, I felt very frightened. I stood rooted to the spot and I wanted to run away. I felt as if I was going to die."

The therapist sets out to challenge her belief that she was going to die by examining the evidence for and against it.

■ How do you know you are going to die when you have a panic attack?
■ You haven't died before, so how can you know what it feels like?

The idea was to make Mary consider an alternative scenario and ask herself critical questions such as:

■ How much do I believe I am going to die when I am having a panic attack and how much do I believe it now?
■ Why do I misinterpret the feelings that make me think I am going to die?
■ How can I control them if I have another attack?

Sitting calmly with her therapist, Mary recognized that a panic attack would not kill her even if it did make her hot and sweaty, make her heart pound and leave her feeling breathless – among other unpleasant things. But this did not remove her fear of further attacks.

The therapist asked Mary to do a test to see if her symptoms may be linked to hyperventilation (rapid breathing). Almost all panic attack sufferers experience hyperventilation. Being aware of hyperventilating and changing your breathing pattern to stop it may help to abort and even prevent panic attacks. (See Further Information: The No Panic website includes instructions about breathing patterns.) The therapist explained that hyperventilating reduces the level of carbon dioxide in the blood, triggering biological mechanisms which set off other panic symptoms.

As part of her homework, Mary used a tape to encourage her to slow down her breathing and to breathe from her stomach not her chest (chest breathing is common among panic attack sufferers). Experiments with both slow and fast breathing convinced Mary that her panic attacks were the result of a vicious circle in which anxiety made her breathe faster.

Reality testing

Graphs are used for "reality testing" – as in the case of the patient featured on page 112). He had a panic attack while preparing his first university lecture and became convinced that he would have another when he faced the class. The therapist asked him to test the validity of this fear by:

- Identifying it and rating it in terms of belief (does he *really* believe it?) on a scale of 1 to 100.
- Working out what it could predict (i.e. the end of his career).
- Devising a homework project to test out his fears.

Rationalizing responses

Thought-provoking event	Feelings	Negative thoughts	Rational response	Result
Presenting first lecture to students.	Anxiety, fear, concern	I'm going to fail. I'll lose my job and finish up on the dole. I'll embarrass the family.	It's only natural to feel nervous. It's actually good to be nervous. It'll keep me on my toes. My employers think I can do it.	Patient re-evaluates his belief rating – giving it a zero score.
		Belief rating: 90%		Belief rating: 0%

The patient collects the evidence (data) to test his fear (the hypothesis) that he would have a panic attack as he presented his first lecture. The grid helped him to see the gulf between his rational and irrational thoughts, resulting in him giving his hypothesis a zero rating. The homework projects that led to this revised rating included presenting the lecture to a small group of friends at college and preparing a report about his colleagues' experience of "performance nerves".

Success therapy

Setting targets to complete routine activities, and thereby encouraging new habits to form is a common CBT technique. Having targets such as to change the bed or to do the weekly supermarket shop may not sound critically important, but as emotional disorders are physically and mentally debilitating, even the most mundane chores can seem impossible to sufferers. Domestic activities account for a large part of our daily routines, and help to give our lives a sense of structure and purpose. Their absence is a detriment to the normal nesting and housekeeping instincts that we have as a successful species, which may explain why people with anxiety disorders often feel isolated or shunned by society.

A "DIY target" could involve preparing a wall to hang wallpaper. New targets should be set as you achieve success. You may believe that you cannot carry out a specific task, but facing up to such beliefs gets right to the heart of what CBT is all about. The therapist may ask: "Are you really sure you cannot do DIY?" or "What's the evidence that you will break down or have a panic attack?" As part of your homework you may be asked to prepare an activity schedule, a graph for every day of the week, in which you can list target activities and time allocated for them.

Keeping a diary

Keeping a regular diary can be hard, but it can help you track your progress – and the inevitable ups and downs. Dividing each daily entry into segments makes it easy to complete. The timekeeper diary records specific daily times and activities, relating them to emotional states. See Michael's diary entry overleaf.

- Date: 22 August 2003
- Situation: Michael has been waiting three days for a client to email confirmation of a job.
- Emotions: convinced that the client is "lining up someone else", he becomes anxious and depressed, fearing the demise of his business. His mind races and he starts experiencing panic.

The diary entries (opposite) show marked improvement in three months of treatment since a patient started keeping a diary.

This is a classic example of "catastrophizing" – making a negative or gloomy assumption without evidence to back it up. Catastrophizing is a common symptom of anxiety disorders and is certainly an indication that Michael is overly critical and anxious without basis. After a period of CBT, rational responses can be filled into the diary entries, with the help of a therapist. In this case the client had not got back to Michael because he'd been unable to confirm dates and times with his colleagues. He actually wanted to offer Michael *more* work. A rational response might have been to assume that Michael's prospective client had his own workloads to juggle. To prevent anxiety spiralling out of control a logical response would have been to phone the client. Use pages 134–135 to create a diary.

The diary entries opposite indicate the results of devoting a significant amount of time to daily routines and involve Beck's concept of mastery and pleasure. This rates activities on a scale of one to five in terms of the pleasure they bring and the extent to which they have been successfully completed. While you would usually agree set tasks or goals with your therapist, the entries could reflect a typical day of someone who is overcoming an anxiety disorder.

Alternatively a simple thoughts and feelings diary may involve "thought catching". In this process, you monitor your feelings, "catch" the accompanying thoughts and record as a "thought diary". This may pinpoint critical differences between your own panic-stricken thoughts and a rational response to a particular anxiety-provoking event.

			Mastery	Pleasure
7–8	am	Got up, dressed, had breakfast	2	0
8–10	am	Housework and other chores	2	0
11–12	am	Morning nap	–	2
12–1	pm	Lunch	3	1
1–3	pm	TV	0	1
4–5	pm	More chores	2	2
5–6	pm	Prepared family meal	2	3
6–7	pm	Family meal	2	3
7–9	pm	TV	0	2

			Mastery	Pleasure
7–8	am	Got up, dressed, had breakfast, cleared up	3	4
8–10	am	Housework and read newspaper (reward)	4	5
11–12	am	Yoga class (reward)	3	5
12–1	pm	Lunch	4	5
1–3	pm	Housework and domestic administration	5	3
4–5	pm	Bookclub meeting	4	4
5–6	pm	Prepare evening meal	5	2
6–7	pm	Eat with family	5	5
7–9	pm	Watch TV with spouse	5	4

Cognitive rehearsal

This exercise involves the role play of anxiety-provoking activities – with help from a therapist. The patient imagines themselves trying to do things they fear are beyond them in order to help identify mental blocks. The therapist might take them through the role-play step by step, asking: "What would you be thinking about at this time?"

In a very typical case, Tony's career was being held back by his fear of speaking to groups of 20 people or more. He became anxious and depressed because his colleagues seemed to speak effortlessly to groups. His therapist asked him to imagine standing in front of an audience just before he was due to start speaking. The therapist then asked him what was going through his mind. What did he fear most? The therapist asked him to write down these negative automatic thoughts, identify the distortions and think of an alternative rational response.

As part of his homework, the therapist asked Tony to prepare a short speech to present both to her in the next session, and to a group of friends or family members. He decided to speak about: "Why public speaking makes me nervous". There was no better way to address his negative thoughts. Moreover, his small audience provided invaluable, confidence-boosting tips, such as using his nerves to inject zip and enthusiasm into what he had to say and having a glass of water in case his mouth went dry.

Negative thought	Distortion	Rational response
I'll tremble and shake. My mind will go blank.	Negative view of self.	It's only natural to feel nervous.
The audience will laugh or feel sorry for me.	Negative view of the world.	I'm a real expert in my field.
I'll finish up getting sacked.	Negative view of the future.	I'm as good as the rest of the team – better than some.

The distortion of thoughts can be likened to a lens which when placed between an anxious person and a situation causes them to "see" the situation wrongly. CBT can help to "clear the vision" of a person with an anxiety disorder.

The walls are closing in

Diana had been agoraphobic for eight years and finally sought help from her GP, a psychiatrist and various complementary therapists. For the previous two years, she had felt she was "more or less coping", with a part-time retail job and an active role in the tennis club, both of which took her out of the house. And then, all within a short time, her children got into trouble at school and her husband had a heart attack.

Her husband recovered, the children's problems were resolved as far as possible, but Diana became increasingly anxious and withdrawn, and eventually felt unable to go out.

Once she had begun CBT therapy, a daily timekeeper diary showed how her life had shrunk, leaving her little to look forward to. After several weeks and various homework assignments, which took her out of the house, she reorganized her daily routine to include pleasure and rewards. Diana soon realized that rewarding herself by slotting pleasure into her routine meant that even the most mundane activities began not to seem so bad.

Diana, 52, housewife

4 CBT and me

"When people will not weed their own minds, they are apt to be overrun with nettles."

Horace Walpole (1717–1797), letter to Lady Ailesbury, 10th July, 1779

How do I get a CBT therapist?

You may not need one. CBT is revolutionizing the treatment of anxiety. It can be accessed via self-help books and innovative computer-based therapy, as well as through a growing number of practitioners. The step care approach, in particular, is a way in which sufferers can help themselves. Professor Isaac Marks, a world authority on anxiety therapy and the author of *Living with Fear,* outlined the principles of the step care approach at a highly acclaimed lecture in 2003 at the Institute of Psychiatry, in London:

■ Step one: Self-help. A patient consulting his doctor with an anxiety disorder may be referred to a self-help group. Alternatively, the doctor may recommend either a self-help book or a computer programme. (See opposite).

■ Step two: Brief therapy. This is offered to patients who do not want self-help or do not respond to it. The therapy consists of either a face-to-face interview or telephone consultation.

■ Step three: Traditional one-to-one CBT therapy. This is offered to people with severe anxiety disorders and to those who did not respond to the first two steps.

While many people will want a traditional one-to-one treatment – either from a CBT therapist, a counsellor or their GP, shame, embarrassment, anxiety, self-consciousness or simply being nervous mean that many people dread the idea of discussing emotional symptoms with any kind of therapist.

Is computer therapy really a good idea?

The idea of a computer CBT programme to beat anxiety may seem strange, but it works for many people. As one report notes: "Software may be more acceptable for some clients. Where problems are of a sensitive nature, or forming trusting relationships is a challenge, computerized psychotherapies (CBT) might offer a preferable alternative." Computer therapy has proven to be an acceptable alternative to face-to-face therapy for those who are able to access it, and as many people now have PCs in the home there is great potential for it to transform anxiety therapy.

Professor Isaac Marks, who helped to develop the FearFighter computerized CBT programme, added: "All the boring questions we [the therapists] ask time and time again, we can leave to the computer. We can reserve our expensively trained skills for those problems the patient cannot have answered by the computer. If and when the patient gets stuck at the computer, they can phone the therapist for advice." The "boring questions" in fact, may even seem less boring when presented in a graphic format.

Designed to tackle phobias and panic disorders, FearFighter has been found to be as effective as CBT delivered entirely by a therapist. It was designed as an extension of conventional one-to-one CBT, not as a replacement, to reduce the time patients need with therapists. Tested in the National Health Service in Britain, it is now used extensively in Europe and the US.

In one case, a 28-year-old woman stopped work for three years as a result of panic attacks. She became severely anxious and depressed and tried medication, without any lasting success. She spent five hours using FearFighter, plus 1.5 hours on screening and back-up with a therapist. Within a month she was much improved, using public transport, and working full-time. Exposure, or facing your fear is key to this target-based programme.

Goals needed to be SMART

S Specific
M Manageable
A Achievable
R Relevant
T Timed

The FearFighter programme highlights the importance of goal-setting in CBT, using the acronym SMART to summarize its approach.

Palmtops – portable access to CBT

The use of palmtops has various advantages for many people, when they are used as a portable reminder to keep CBT diaries up to date. Developed specifically for palmtop computers, *The Stress Manager* © is programmed to beep four times during the day to remind users to record the percentage of time in an hour they have spent worrying, the number of acute (higher than five on a 0 to 10 scale) anxiety spells they have had since last using their computer, and their highest rate of anxiety in the previous hour (on a 0 to 10 scale). For the first two days the computer can be programmed to beep every waking hour to remind users to log their anxiety. The idea is to familiarize users with early warning signs of anxiety.[3]

The evening diary beeps at 10pm with a series of questions about average and highest levels of anxiety and percentage of time spent worrying during the day. Users are asked whether anything that they are worried about resulted in their most feared outcome coming true that day. If they say "no", they are asked to take a moment to consider all the time and energy they spent worrying about something that didn't happen. If they say "yes", they are asked to rate if they coped better than they predicted. If they did cope better they are reminded their ability to cope is usually better than they predict. If they did not cope better than predicted, they are asked to imagine looking back on the event in five years and ask themselves if the outcome was so important their future depended upon it.

The programme has a relaxation module which includes six different versions of progressive muscle relaxation, breathing exercises and a pleasant imagery exercise which can be activated at any time. The idea that constant beeps is intrusive is countered by separate studies, which suggest the opposite – that they can be reassuring.

Computerized CBT

A man diagnosed with agoraphobia and obsessive-compulsive tendencies could not leave home alone except to go to his best friend's home or other safe places. The 30-year-old used a "graded exposure" computer programme, which included compiling a "hierarchy" of the least to the most feared situations. He was exposed to them in a number of graded steps. Each grade was designed to stimulate a dose of fear large enough to be meaningful, but small enough to enable the sufferer to "stay with it" for long enough to realize there was no rational basis for concern. Graded exposure is the most common kind of exposure programme.

The first of the 12 weekly computer sessions explained the programme structure, outlined theories about the cause of phobias, and emphasized the critical importance of assuming responsibility for completing the coursework.

Equally importantly, it offered hope. The patient was also given an audio relaxation tape each day before the next session.

The computer asked the patient to *imagine* himself facing his fears. Four items from the "fear hierarchy" were presented in each session before he confronted them in real life as part of his between-session homework. The computer recommended appropriate graded responses to his real life fears based on his reaction to the "imagined" exposure.

The man made a dramatic improvement, during six months of follow up. Setting up in business as a delivery man, he was able to go where he wanted by himself and became increasingly confident. Friends described him as "a changed man".

Anon

START

Would you like to do the CBT program?
1 Yes 2 No
3 Practise relaxing

↓

Enter your anxiety level now: 1–10

0-1-2-3-4-5-6-7-8-9-10
relaxation   discomfort

↓

Examine the evidence to support your fear.

↓

Rate on a scale of 1–10 the likelihood your fears will come true.
0 = not at all likely
10 = will happen

↓

Are there equally likely ways of viewing this situation?
1) Yes 2) No

→

You identified catastrophizing – anticipating worst outcome despite low probabilities.

↑

If 4...

↑

0) none of these errors
1) filtering
2) black-white thinking
3) mind-reading
4) catastrophizing
5) control fallacies
6) personalization
7) overgeneralization
8) emotional reasoning

↑

Did you notice any logical errors?
(Press nine for different types of errors)

↑

Would you interpret the situation differently if it was another person experiencing it? 1) Yes 2) No

Examine the realistic odds with respect to what is frightening you.

↓

Are there other possible outcomes for this feared event? 1) Yes 2) No

↓

Imagine your worst fear came true. Enter the extent of the damage on a scale of 0–10

↓

Think of the best possible outcome. Record the extent of the damage for the best outcome.

↓

Is the catastrophic or the best outcome likely to occur?
1) Catastrophic
2) Best outcome

→

What is your anxiety level now?

0-1-2-3-4-5-6-7-8-9-10
relaxation   discomfort

END

↑

Remember it is wise to anticipate probable dangers; not every conceivable catastrophe.

↑

For example: I have encountered a similar situation and the outcome was positive.

or Even if my worst fear comes true it would not be the end of the world.

↑

Challenge your catastrophic beliefs.

What about other treatment options?

One possibility is to join a group therapy telephone course which may consist of weekly sessions over three to four months. Groups of up to six people, plus a leader, are linked via a teleconference link (see the case history on page 127). Sessions usually last an hour. Courses are run as far as possible on conventional CBT lines – with homework assignments and goal setting.

The challenge for course leaders in such self-help groups is to reconcile the weekly agenda to the need to give everyone (from the shy and reticent to the more talkative and vocal) ample opportunity to contribute. Ideally, leaders should be specially trained in teleconferencing skills and have been treated with CBT as part of their own treatment. Each week will probably be given over to a specific topic such as understanding fear or anxiety or keeping a diary.

Experience suggests that it is better for groups to feel their own way, rather than to have continuing dependence on a leader. Inevitably some groups are more successful than others and all have to go through a trial and error process to discover what works best for its members. It is possible for groups to set up self-facilitating befriending groups when group CBT ends. Such groups can offer another effective means of therapy. They may comprise weekly face-to-face sessions or telephone sessions.

The flow chart opposite demonstrates the progression of screens in the computerized CBT package Stress Manager ©. Each box represents a new screen, which appear when the patient responds to questions on their Palmtop computer. In this example, the error of thinking leading to anxiety is one of "catastrophizing" a situation.

Bibliotherapy – healing by books

Self-help or mutual aid is a fast growing area among the health-care options available in the modern world. The phenomenal increase in self-help implies that health-care professionals alone cannot provide the level of understanding and support that people need – especially in the treatment of anxiety, the most common emotional disorder. The explosion in the demand for "bibliotherapy" or self-help books has added a major new dimension to the support available.

There is nothing new about bibliotherapy – the words "Medicine for the Soul" were inscribed over the door of the Library at Thebes in Ancient Greece. But we have had to wait until the twenty-first century to see doctors actually prescribing bibliotherapy. In a pioneering UK scheme, some GPs have been writing prescriptions for books about generalized anxiety disorder, social phobia and other emotional problems. A list of 30 books is being made available in public libraries to patients with mild to moderate problems.[4]

This endorsement follows research showing that one self-help book, *The Feeling Good Handbook* by David Burns had a 70 per cent success rate.[5] This is similar to conventional one-to-one therapy or drugs in some cases. Some patients with severe or chronic disorders will still need the help of a therapist; others may combine bibliotherapy and drugs – or even bibliotherapy, drugs and conventional one-to-one therapy.

Bibliotherapy for anxiety disorders is not restricted to books about fear and worry. Reading can be highly therapeutic in its own right – as can writing. CBT involves keeping a diary in a rather formal way, but descriptive writing can provide an invaluable focus. As one woman put it, "writing gives me...a tangible anchor for my turbulent thoughts".[6]

Group CBT using teleconference via telephone link

There's a one-year waiting list for standard CBT in our area, but I was able to access group therapy within six weeks of applying. It was really helpful – 14 one-hour weekly sessions, all free apart from the small cost of the relaxation tape and call costs. A real bargain.

There were six of us from all over the country, plus the group leader, all with different types of phobias and anxieties. It made me really appreciate that I wasn't alone, and, of course, talking is very easy. The phone is a link to the outside world from the safety net of your own home. It's also anonymous – so there's no need to worry about having a panic attack and looking foolish in front of other people.

We kept diaries and did homework – just as in conventional CBT. We began by introducing ourselves – first names, occupations, ages and problems. I'm 57 and have a history of anxiety and panic attacks and agoraphobia. The group leader had been an anxiety sufferer herself.

We discussed our goals with her. My first goal was to get to the corner shop, then to the chemist's across the road and finally to the main shops, two or three hundreds yards away. It's not so long ago that it seemed like a million miles away, but I now go on the bus twice a week for a computer course. I couldn't have managed this before.

At the end, six of us decided to keep in touch by setting up a self-facilitating, befriending group. This didn't really work as we found out we needed a leader to keep an eye on the session and structure the agenda. There are now only three of us left. We still have a conference-call every fortnight; it doesn't achieve much – but I'm really glad I did the course.

Joyce, 57, housewife

What are the success rates of CBT?

Success rates are still hard to monitor, though the following gives an idea of the effectiveness in the context of different disorders. Much of the conclusions are based on meta-analysis – a statistical technique which combines the findings from different studies to measure overall effect – as presented in several books cited below covering the benefits of CBT.

Generalized anxiety disorder

CBT has a "unique efficacy" in the treatment of generalized anxiety disorder, according to Anthony Roth and Peter Fonagy in *What Works for Whom?* [7], the internationally acclaimed "bible" of psychotherapy research. They say that:

- Research shows "good evidence of efficacy" in CBT given by experienced therapists. Two-thirds to three-quarters of patients may show "clinically significant improvement" after six months.

- These effects are markedly greater than those from other types of treatment such as analytic therapy, non-directive counselling, applied relaxation training and biofeedback.

One of the big challenges in treating anxiety is finding successful treatments with long-lasting effects. Roth and Fonagy highlight studies in which the benefits of CBT were found to be significantly longer lasting than those of other treatments. For example, 81 per cent of CBT patients were at least "moderately improved" after one study,[8] compared to 80 per cent who received anxiety management training (AMT) and 74 per cent who received analytical psychotherapy (AP). Six months later, 76 per cent of the CBT patients were still at least "moderately improved", compared with 49 per cent of the AMP group and 42 per cent of the AP group.

Nonetheless, there is concern about the lasting effects of all treatments. One of the central messages in this book is that CBT is not just for the duration of the treatment. Just as an athlete has to carry on exercising to retain their fitness, a CBT patient or client should carry on "exercising", using the techniques of CBT on a life-long basis to challenge negative, dysfunctional thinking.

Panic disorder with or without agoraphobia

In *Cognitive Therapy for Depression and Anxiety*, the authors Ivy-Marie Blackburn and Kate Davidson report that cognitive techniques appear to improve panic symptoms and they cite evidence that the benefits last longer than those of drug therapy. In their study this is particularly evident at 15 months follow-up. In addition:

■ Combinations of cognitive treatment and exposure to the fear-provoking stimulus seem to be effective in treating panic disorder with agoraphobia in two-thirds of cases; in sufferers of panic disorder without agoraphobia, about 85 per cent improve. Relaxation therapy may be a useful addition to treatment.

■ The benefits of treatment are, on the whole, maintained with psychological therapies, but are less consistent with drugs where gains tend to stop when treatment stops.

Specific/simple phobia

A high percentage of specific phobias, perhaps as many as 75–80 per cent, are effectively treated by exposure therapy. Interestingly, studies have shown that adding cognitive techniques seems to add little benefit to treatment.

Social phobia

Cognitive and behavioural approaches have demonstrated moderate to strong effects in sufferers of social phobia. Cognitive therapy has been found to enhance the effects of exposure treatment.

Obsessive-compulsive disorder (OCD)

Treatment is, unfortunately not a simple process, however the following present a picture which is not altogether disheartening:

- Exposure treatment in combination with so called "response prevention" to block obsessive ideas or compulsive behaviour has been found to produce a 30–50 per cent improvement in 75 per cent of patients according to Roth and Fonagy.

- Cognitive therapy has also been found to be an effective addition to exposure.

In his book, *Staying Sane*, Dr Raj Persaud explains that one way to treat a patient who feels compelled to shower up to 30 times a day would be to deliberately make him dirty and then prevent him from washing. He says: "Such treatment may sound cruel, but it is important to remember that patients are only very gradually exposed to their fears. So before they are exposed to the most frightening stimuli, they will have started with things that only cause a little anxiety. This treatment has proved to be effective in even the most severe cases, and research has definitely shown that exposure to the feared situation is crucial for recovery from OCD."

So, on balance, does CBT have a lot to recommend it?

As we observed earlier, CBT is significantly changing our perspectives about the way we view ourselves and our problems. However, though it is now 50 years or so since Aaron Beck started developing CBT, it is only recently that it has come centre stage. It has already established itself as a powerful treatment in depression therapy. Leading practitioners believe that it will become equally prominent in the treatment of some anxiety disorders and indeed the numbers of people asking for treatment are continuing to rise. It also provides another option for treatment in a range of disorders where the most effective treatment is one that has been personalized or tailored to the needs of the individual.

Nevertheless, research has produced conflicting results. Some studies – in social phobia, for example – have concluded that CBT works; others have found no benefit. This is not as odd as it appears: medical research is full of contradictions. A wrong hypothesis, a statistical flaw, faulty methodology may all affect results. This is why it is important to duplicate research by testing the same basic hypotheses in different studies. It is only by adopting this approach that research can develop a strong "evidence base" for treatment guidelines.

Developing this base is particularly difficult in disorders that are hard to treat, or where treatment is rarely completed such as obsessive-compulsive disorder. As an individual starting CBT for *any kind* of anxiety disorder, it is important to realize you will become part of a similar trial and error process. CBT will not help everyone with general anxiety, but by *using your brain* you will be able to increase the chances of it helping you.

Choosing a therapist

The further information section gives details on how to find a therapist. When choosing a therapist it may help to seek answers to these questions before starting treatment:

- What are your qualifications – are you fully qualified?
- What professional associations do you belong to?
- How much do you charge?
- Do you offer CBT as standard practice?
- How long have you been practising?
- What areas do you specialize in?
- Where do you practise?
- Will what I say be confidential?*
- Do you subscribe to a particular code of ethics?
- How long is the treatment likely to take?
- What happens if I feel I'm making no progress after, say, three or four sessions?
- How often will we see one another?
- Will it be OK if I call between sessions – will you charge for this?
- What about any charges for cancelled appointments and holidays?

*Establish whether the therapist will be discussing your case with a supervisor or any other third party.

Notes

_____
_____
_____
_____
_____
_____
_____
_____
_____
_____
_____
_____
_____
_____
_____
_____
_____
_____
_____
_____
_____
_____
_____
_____
_____
_____

Use this page to take down important information when considering a therapist. You can consult the guide opposite for a quick reminder of the questions you should ask at an initial appointment, in a letter or over the phone.

Thoughts and feelings diary

Use this diary to help record your progress, before during or after CBT treatment. You can also use it to monitor your periods of anxiety (see pages 113–116).

Time	Monday	Tuesday	Wednesday
7am–8am			
8am–9am			
9am–10am			
10am–11am			
11am–12pm			
12pm–1pm–			
1pm–2pm–			
2pm–3pm–			
3pm–4pm–			
4pm–6pm–			
6pm–8pm–			

Thursday	Friday	Saturday	Sunday

Food and mood diary

Use these pages to record any occasions when you feel that you are eating as a response to emotional or anxiety-provoking situations.

Mood	Monday	Tuesday	Wednesday	Thursday	Friday	Saturday	Sunday
Happy							
Tired							
Angry							
Sad							
Anxious							
Lonely							
Other (please specify)							

Monday	Tuesday	Wednesday	Thursday	Friday	Saturday	Sunday

5 The final story

"Our remedies oft in ourselves do lie,
Which we ascribe to heaven."

William Shakespeare (1564–1616), *All's Well That Ends Well*, **Act 1, scene i**

This book describes modern treatment methods and provides advice on treating anxiety – the most common mental health problem in the twenty-first century. But the modern age does not have a monopoly on good advice. In the year 4BC, the Spanish born Roman statesman and philosopher Seneca observed: "There are more things to alarm us than to harm us, and we suffer more often in apprehension than reality." He may have been one of the first people to expound the principles of cognitive behaviour therapy (CBT).

Benjamin Franklin (1706–1790), US scientist, publisher and diplomat, advised: "Do not anticipate trouble, or worry about what may never happen. Keep in the sunlight." In the late twentieth century, the self-help group PAX (Panic Attacks and Anxiety, an information service set up for sufferers of panic and anxiety) adopted this slogan: "Today is the tomorrow you worried about yesterday."

Yet, despite persistent good advice over the centuries, the need for this book is as strong as ever. Why? The answer is that "normal", everyday anxiety is so common we feel we should not make a fuss about it. The problem comes when we fail to distinguish between everyday anxiety and forms that are potentially disabling. Even if we make such a distinction, we may not act because of the stigma of anxiety, or because we do not want to admit the problem – even to ourselves. A key message of this book is that it is vital to acknowledge any problem and seek treatment.

In her book *An Aspect of Fear,* Grace Shepherd speaks out about how fear of rejection can inhibit this process. She explains: "This rejection feels like the final judgement. So in order to avoid even thinking about that, we stifle our fear – and press on. When we do this, we shut off part of who we are, or divide ourselves into parts that we can accept and parts we cannot...Fear is not a sin. It is not a failure. It is simply a sign that we are alive." [9] Acknowledging a problem is the first step to treatment and recovery – but treatment does not guarantee cure, far from it. Using your brain to beat panic and anxiety means learning about the pros and cons of different treatments and working out what is best – for you. For example, drugs can be effective as a short-term emergency measure, but you will not resolve underlying causes of panic and anxiety problems in this way.

CBT provides a proven means of identifying and resolving psychological problems, but it is not as simple as popping a pill – it demands commitment and hard work. Some people have difficulty managing the homework because they are not used to writing, and feel shy or embarrassed from lack of practice or fear of spelling mistakes. Other people intellectualize their problems, without taking account of their feelings, or try to block their emotions, or claim prematurely that they do not need further treatment.

Nevertheless, the benefits outweigh the difficulties and lifestyle measures such as diet, exercise and social support can also help to remove the sharp edges, but, again, these demand discipline. Most people draw a sharp distinction between lifestyle and treatment. This is not surprising when lifestyle is for life, while treatment usually lasts only a few weeks. But for the most effective treatment CBT helps manage disorders for life; not just in the short-term. Using CBT techniques on a regular basis, for example, can help to alert you to any negative "automatic thoughts" signalling a recurrence of any problem. You will, in time, develop your own built-in personal "alarm system" and, as a result, be able to minimize the effects of anxiety by taking preventative action.

Part Three
Resources

1. Treatment

This section is intended only as a reference point and a brief description of the more commonly prescribed treatments by GPs in the UK. Other treatments, such as homeopathy and holistic remedies, are not listed here – as there are too many to mention them individually. For a useful starting point for complementary medicine see the contacts in 'Further information' page 165. Please note that in the case of herbal medicine, there are as many disreputable places selling quack cures as there are reputable ones. This is not to discredit the many remedies which have been proven to work, (see the summaries in Part One pages 69–77), but as with any treatment taken it is useful to research your options thoroughly. Research could take the form of personal recommendations as well as the Internet which has a wealth of information – though be sure to check qualifications and membership of recognized standard-setting bodies – ask your GP's advice and talk to your practitioner about costs and time involved before buying any remedy or undertaking treatment.

The name game

Entries in the directory are listed under their generic name and where applicable a brand name is also given. The former describes the drug's active chemical ingredient; the latter is chosen by the manufacturers. For example, Xanax is the brand name of the tranquillizer alprazolam. Manufacturers try to make brand names catchy and easy for prescribing doctors and patients to remember. Several different brand name drugs may contain the same active ingredient. Doctors are encouraged to prescribe the generic versions because they are cheaper than, and as effective as, brands.

Why the cost difference? The answer is that a new drug is marketed under a patented brand name in the hope that it will capture a big share of the highly competitive pharmaceutical market while the patent is in force. When the patent expires, other companies can produce the same medicine, but not under the original brand name. A "copycat" product may differ in shape and size to the original, but the active ingredient in a generic product will be identical. Generic manufacturers do not have to meet the research and development costs of bringing a new drug to market, which explains the inflated price of brand name drugs.

Anti-anxiety drugs are also known as "anxiolytics".

Limitations of drugs

No medicine is totally safe and your medication may cause unwanted side effects. Any decision to take a drug means weighing up potential benefits against potential risks. Involving patients in this process is now seen as the best option and is entirely expected by doctors, so return to your doctor if a drug causes troublesome side effects. There may be an alternative drug you can take. Trial and error is often the key to successful treatment.

Twenty questions

This directory begins with 20 questions you may find useful to ask your doctor or pharmacist – you may not need to ask them all – and it is useful to read them through and make a note of which ones are appropriate for you to help you get the maximum possible benefit from treatment. The more you know about your treatment the better:

"You are not challenging a doctor's competence when you ask…questions: in fact, you will be showing that you are interested in the treatment and want to achieve the best possible result."

Michael Orme and Susanna Graham Jones, *Medicine: The Self Help Guide*, Viking, 1988

■ What sort of drug is it?

■ What does it do?

■ What will happen if I don't take it?

■ Is there a non-drug alternative?

■ What else can I do to get better, in addition to taking the drug?

■ When should I take it?

■ Will my doseage change over time?

■ How many days or weeks does it take to work?

■ How long will it be before it *starts* to work?

■ Will it make me drowsy or sleepy?

■ What about other possible side effects?

■ What can I do about any side effects that do occur?

■ Will I still be able to drive/use machinery?

■ Can I take other drugs with this one?

■ Are there any foods or drinks I should avoid?

■ Will I need to come back to the surgery for a check-up?

■ Where should I keep this drug?

■ What about repeat prescriptions?

■ Are there alternative drugs if this one doesn't work?

■ Where can I find more information about this drug?

Benzodiazepines

These act on special sites in the brain known as benzodiazepine receptors. Benzodiazepine drugs bind to the receptors. This increases the effects of a natural brain chemical called gamma-aminobutyric acid (GABA) which slows down activity within the brain.

History The first benzodiazepine, chlordiazepoxide (Librium), was launched in 1960. Promoted as "safer, non-addictive alternatives" to the highly addictive barbiturates, the benzodiazepines nevertheless also proved to be extremely addictive, and have been grossly over-prescribed. The best known is Valium, once the world's most widely prescribed drug.

Effectiveness Benzodiazepines are fast acting (usually within an hour or less) and can have a marked calming effect, but they are recommended only for severe, disabling or extremely distressing anxiety; and then, usually, only at the lowest possible dose for the least possible time. *The Maudsley 2003 Prescribing Guidelines* generally recommends a four-week maximum course, but says: "A very small number of patients with severely disabling anxiety may benefit from long term treatment and these patients should not be denied treatment".[1]

In general, tranquillizers of this type are reported to have no proven effectiveness beyond four months and in fact the risk of addiction increases significantly if you take a benzodiazepine for more than a few weeks. Many specialists maintain anxiety can almost always be treated successfully without benzodiazepines.

Three related problems diminish their effectiveness:

- *Tolerance:* Over time the effects of the drugs diminish as the body develops tolerance to them.

- *Addiction:* (see below).

- *Withdrawal effects:* (see below).

Side effects These include drowsiness and tiredness, impaired memory and concentration and ataxia (shaky movements – particularly unsteadiness on the feet), especially in the elderly. Less common side effects include aggressive outbursts and visual disturbances. Alcohol and other sedative drugs should be avoided while taking benzodiazepines as they dramatically enhance the toxicity of the drug. Fatal overdoses have occurred when benzodiazepine is combined with other chemical compounds. Always consult your doctor when taking medication in combination with other compounds.

Stopping Knowing when and how to stop taking a benzodiazepine is critical. Over a period of a week or so of taking the drug your body will adapt to it and it will need to re-adapt when you stop taking it. Stopping the drug abruptly can cause "rebound anxiety" or, in more severe cases, withdrawal symptoms. Ironically, these may be virtually identical to your initial anxiety symptoms and may include aches and pains, agitation, appetite loss, insomnia, palpitations, restlessness and sweating.

If you have been taking some benzodiazepines for less than two weeks, you may be able to stop them safely without any need to gradually taper the doses downwards. Check with your doctor about your particular drug. Benzodiazepines are divided into three groups according to their "duration of action" (how long they work for):

■ Long acting (40 hours plus)

■ Medium acting (10–40 hours)

■ Short acting (less than 10 hours)

Short-acting compounds tend to have more severe withdrawal effects than long acting ones, but they are prescribed because they are less likely to cause "a hangover" the next day.

The directory lists the duration of action of each benzodiazepine and its potential addiction risk. Switching from a short-acting to a longer-acting benzodiazepine can reduce the impact of withdrawal.

Comments Prescribed at the right level for the right time, these drugs are safe for most people. Different benzodiazepines have different effects. For example, diazepam is a strong muscle relaxant, while alprazolam has been reported to have an antidepressant effect.

Generic or chemical name Diazepam

Brand name Valium

Uses Anxiety. Insomnia. Somnambulism (sleep-walking). Acute alcohol withdrawal. Occasionally prescribed for panic attacks.

Comment Intramuscular or slow intravenous injection formulations are sometimes administered for severe acute anxiety, acute panic attacks and acute alcohol withdrawal; suppositories for anxiety; rectal solutions for acute anxiety and agitation. Diazepam is also a highly effective muscle relaxant.

Duration of action Long acting

Addiction risk Moderate

Generic or chemical name Alprazolam

Brand name Xanax

Uses Anxiety (short-term use only)

Comment Long acting. More potent than other benzodiazepines. Can have intense withdrawal symptoms, and is especially likely to cause addiction if taken in large doses for prolonged periods. Initially, alprazolam was claimed to have a unique effect in treating panic attacks, but later studies suggested that other benzodiazepines in high doses were also capable of suppressing symptoms. Alprazolam has also been reported to have an antidepressant effect, but according to Alyson Bond and Malcolm H. Lader the benzodiazepines have only a "minimal" effect on depression.[2]

Duration of action Medium

Addiction risk Fairly high

Generic or chemical name Chlordiazepoxide

Brand name Librium

Uses Anxiety

Comment The first "benzo", chlordiazepoxide was launched in 1960, after being discovered accidentally by Polish American scientist Leo Sternbach as he was clearing out his laboratory.

Duration of action Long

Addiction risk Moderate

Generic or chemical name Clorazepate

Brand name Tranxene

Uses Anxiety.

Duration of action Long

Addiction risk Moderate

Generic or chemical name Lorazapam

Brand name Ativan

Uses Anxiety and insomnia

Comment Can have especially intense withdrawal symptoms.

Duration of action Short (Medium according to Bond and Lader [3])

Addiction risk Fairly high

Generic or chemical name Oxazepam

Brand name n/a

Comment Less potent than some other benzodiazepines and requires a larger dose.

Uses Anxiety

Duration of action: Short to medium

Addiction risk Fairly high

Antidepressant drugs

Until recently, benzodiazepine tranquillizers were the main drugs used in the treatment of anxiety. Antidepressants are now seen as the first choice drug treatment.

There is a lot of conflicting information about how long antidepressants take to work. Some reports say that that the benefits may not be apparent for several weeks; others suggest that they begin in the first week. A lot may depend on your age and your particular problem. Older people may have to wait longer to feel a therapeutic effect, while people with panic disorder may have to wait four to six weeks to feel a significant effect. Seek advice from your doctor about how long it is likely to be before your treatment starts working.

Antidepressants are sometimes prescribed in combination with benzodiazepines which have an almost immediate effect; however the latter should not usually be used for long periods because of the addiction risk (see pages 64–67).

The question of whether antidepressants are also addictive is highly controversial. The debate centres on the definition of "addiction". According to the medical definition, an addictive drug causes "tolerance", meaning that the brain needs more and more of the drug to maintain the desired effect. Antidepressants (unlike drugs such as heroin or cocaine) do not create this kind of craving, but they can give rise to "discontinuation syndrome" where symptoms occur when a patient comes off antidepressants.

These symptoms may be new or similar to those of some of the illness, and usually subside within a few days. In some cases, however, they are reported to persist with traumatic results. The discontinuation syndrome affects approximately a third of patients coming off antidepressant therapy, according to one report.[4]

Antidepressants and Children

In 2005 The UK National Institute Health and Clinical Excellence (published guidelines calling on doctors to restrict antidepressa prescribing to children and you people. Following reports that a depressants may trigger suicida feelings among young people, was said to mark a watershed children's mental health, shiftin emphasis from drugs to psycho therapy. About 40,000 children UK were estimated to be taking depressants for depression, an and other problems. These guic focused specifically on depress but were also expected to set standards for treating anxiety re disorders among children. The lines stated that children and ye people with moderate to severe depression should be offered, a first line treatment, a specific psychological therapy. Also, ant depressants should not be give children or young people with moderate to severe depression except when in combination w psychological therapy, and shou be given at all to children with r depression.

Tricyclic and related antidepressant drugs

Name Their name is derived from the three linked six-sided rings that make up their molecular structure. In some drugs one ring is seven-sided.

History Discovered by accident in the late 1950s, the first tricyclic antidepressant (TCA) was imipramine. Amitriptyline followed soon after.

Effectiveness TCAs are among the most effective of all antidepressants, but between 10 and 20 per cent of patients don't respond to TCAs and related antidepressants. [5]

Side effects Not everyone experiences side effects, but they are common and can be severe, especially in the first week or two of treatment. They tend to disappear thereafter – underlining the importance of sticking with the treatment during any initial difficult period. Common side effects include:

- blurred vision
- constipation
- difficulty passing water
- drowsiness
- feeling faint
- increased appetite
- loss of libido
- rapid heartbeat.

Initial low doses may reduce side effects, but increase the time the drug takes to work. TCAs can interfere with diabetes control and heart action and exacerbate epilepsy. Combining TCAs with other drugs can also create problems. It is best to check potential interactions with your doctor.

Overdose Seek immediate medical advice: overdose is extremely dangerous. TCAs can impair ability to drive or use machinery.

Stopping them TCAs should not be stopped abruptly. They are not addictive, but can cause unpleasant withdrawal effects such as insomnia, nausea, panic and vomiting. Reducing the dose gradually over several weeks can prevent or reduce bad effects. Seek advice from your doctor.

Comment The British National Formulary (BNF), advises that although newer drugs are better tolerated than older ones the difference is too small to justify always choosing one of the newer drugs as the first line treatment.[6] Tricyclics are therefore still an important prescribing option especially in cases of anxiety with depression.

Generic or chemical name Clomipramine
Brand name Anafranil, Anafranil SR
Uses Panic disorders, phobias, irrational fears, obsessive-compulsive disorder, narcolepsy (an uncontrollable sleep-inducing condition), depressive illness (especially if sedation is required).
Comment A powerful drug and the first (1990) to be approved by the US Food and Drugs Administration for treating obsessive-compulsive disorder. It is reported to result in significant reduction in OCD symptoms for patients who can tolerate it – but many patients stop it because of severe side effects. It is not a first choice antidepressant but it is, however, widely used to treat "refractory" cases (depression unresponsive to other treatments).

Generic or chemical name Dosulepin /Dothiepin
Brand name Prothiaden
Uses Depression, especially with anxiety and insomnia.
Comment May relieve anxiety within a few days, but take several weeks to achieve a full effect. It has a sedative effect which can be strong.

Generic or chemical name Trimipramine

Brand name Surmontil

Uses Depression, particularly if sedation is needed to treat anxiety, agitation or disturbed sleep.

Comment Another frequently prescribed treatment. It has a strong sedative effect and usually resolves sleep problems within 24 hours. A true antidepressant effect may occur quickly – within 7 to 10 days.

Generic or chemical name Trazodone

Brand name Molipaxin

Uses Depression (especially if sedation is required) and anxiety.

Comment One of the more sedative of available antidepressant drugs, it has hardly any cholinergic, or nerve-blocking effects. Thus, it is less likely to cause symptoms such as dry mouth, blurred vision, constipation and urinary problems. Also reported to be relatively safe for people with heart problems. Priapism (a permanent erection) is a rare complication, in which case it should be discontinued immediately. Its use as a sedative for sleep disorders has been questioned. Alyson J. Bond and Malcolm Lader say it is "unpredictable and unreliable and should be used only to treat the primary illness of depression."[7]

Selective Serotonin Reuptake Inhibitors

Name Selective serotonin reuptake inhibitors (SSRIs) act by blocking reuptake (re-absorption) of one neurotransmitter – serotonin.

History The first SSRI, Prozac, launched in 1988, became the world's biggest selling psychotherapeutic medicine. SSRIs mark a major advance because they are a lot safer and easier to take than the older tricyclic antidepressants.

Side effects SSRIs cause less drowsiness and are less likely to cause dry mouth and blurred vision than other antidepressants. Common side effects are restlessness, insomnia, diarrhoea, nausea and vomiting. Doctors have found that about half of patients experience some SSRI-related sexual dysfunction. Psychiatrist Dr Tim Cantopher has commented: "It may last for as long as you take the tablets (plus a short period while the drug gets out of your system). It's not you, it's the tablets and some other antidepressants can do the same thing." [8]

Generic or chemical name Citalopram
Brand name Cipramil
Uses Depression and panic disorder

Generic or chemical name Escitalopram
Brand name Cipralex
Uses Depression and panic disorder.
Comment Newer drug which may have fewer side effects than other SSRIs and be more potent.

Generic or chemical name Fluoxetine
Brand name Prozac
Uses Depression, bulimia nervosa, obsessive-compulsive disorder (OCD).
Comment Fluoxetine has a long half life, one to three days after acute (short-term) therapy and four to six days after chronic (long-term) therapy. "Half life" is the time it takes for a drug in the blood to decrease to half of its original dose. This means that traces of fluoxetine will linger in your body for much longer than other SSRIs – for up to six weeks. This could be bad news if you develop side effects. Fluoxetine may also decrease appetite and have a slight stimulant effect.

Generic or chemical name Fluvoxamine
Brand name Faverin

Uses Depression and obsessive-compulsive disorder (OCD).

Comment First SSRI launched in worldwide market in 1983; first approved by US Food and Drugs Administration for OCD treatment.

Generic or chemical name Paroxetine
Brand name Seroxat
Uses Depression, obsessive-compulsive disorder (OCD), panic disorder, social phobia, post-traumatic disorder, anxiety.
Comment Provoked controversy over claims it is addictive – a claim the manufacturers vehemently deny. First SSRI approved by the US Food and Drugs Administration for the treatment of panic disorder and social phobia.

Generic or chemical name Sertraline
Brand name Lustral
Uses Depression, including accompanying symptoms of anxiety; obsessive-compulsive disorder, post-traumatic stress disorder.
Comment Usually has a slight stimulant effect.

"Designer" antidepressants

Dual action serotonin and noradrenaline (norepinephrine) reuptake inhibitors (SSNRIs) may help patients who do not respond to SSRIs – which only work on the serotonin system. Old-fashioned tricyclic antidepressants also work on both the serotonin and noradrenaline systems, but SSRIs and SSNRIs are less dangerous in overdose and have fewer side effects. Venlafaxine (brand names: Efexor and Efexor XL) is the first SSNRI. It is licensed to treat generalized anxiety disorder (GAD) and depression.

Mirtazapine (Remeron) is a new kind of antidepressant. Reports suggest that it may also be effective in the treatment of panic disorder, generalized anxiety disorder, obsessive-compulsive disorder and post-traumatic stress disorder. The first antidepressant of its kind, it works by preventing noradrenaline and serotonin binding to receptors found on nerve cells. This has a mood-lightening effect.

Anti-psychotic agents

Anti-psychotic drugs are normally used to treat people with psychotic illnesses such as schizophrenia. In these illnesses people lose touch with reality and are unable to distinguish between what is happening in the outside world and in their internal world of muddled thoughts and feelings. Antipsychotic drugs dampen the effects of dopamine, a neurotransmitter which controls muscle movement, thought and emotion. Drugs used to treat anxiety include risperidone (Risperdal), trifluoperazine (Stelazine), olanzapine (Zyprexa) and quetiapine (Seroquel).

You should only be prescribed one of these drugs if your symptoms become severe or if other treatments fail. Four out of ten patients taking trifluoperazine for anxiety disorders complain that it makes them drowsy [9] and a quarter are reported to develop dry mouth, blurred vision or constipation. [10] In rare cases long-term use of antipsychotic medication can cause tardive dyskinesia – loss of limb control. [11]

Beta blockers

Beta blockers inhibit the stimulating action of noradrenaline, the main "fight or flight" hormone which primes the body for rapid and vigorous action. This suppresses the *physical* symptoms of anxiety disorders such as a rapid heartbeat, fast breathing, tremors and sweating. Beta blockers are predominantly used to treat angina and high blood pressure, and also migraine headaches. They probably have no direct effect on emotional symptoms such as worry and fear.

Side effects associated with beta blockers can be extreme – such as heart failure. But anxiety treatment involves only small doses compared with other uses and is unlikely to cause problems. Nonetheless, beta blockers are powerful drugs and should be avoided if you have a heart condition – check with your doctor if you are unsure. They also should not be taken by people with asthma and they interact with many other medications. They can, for example, intensify the effects of benzodiazepine tranquillizers and block the therapeutic benefits of anti-asthma medications. Beta blockers prescribed for anxiety include propranolol (brand name Inderal) and oxpenolol (brand name Trasicor).

Azapirones

This family of drugs comprises a unique anti-anxiety agent called buspirone (Buspar). We still do not know exactly how it works, but it acts on the serotonin system and is used to treat refractory (treatment resistant) depression, although clinical experience is very limited.[12] It takes up to two weeks to start working and up to three or four weeks to achieve its full effect. The American psychiatrist David D. Burns comments: "It is thought to be only somewhat effective for generalized anxiety and social phobia and less effective for other forms of anxiety such as panic attacks or obsessive-compulsive disorder." [13]

One clear benefit is that buspirone seems not to be addictive, and is reported to be useful in the treatment of people with a history of addiction. However, it does not help to relieve benzodiazepine withdrawal symptoms. It is sometimes combined with antidepressants in the Prozac drug family because these drugs can produce an initial increase in anxiety.

Antihistamines

These drugs are the most widely used in the treatment of allergic reactions. They are sub-divided according to their chemical structure. Some have mild sedative and anti-anxiety properties. These include chlorpheniramine (Piriton), hydroxyzine (Atarax) and promethazine (Phenergan). An advantage of anti-histamines is that they are not addictive and do not cause withdrawal symptoms.

2. Further information

Part One

Useful contacts

No Panic

93 Brands Farm Way

Telford

Shropshire

TF3 2JQ

Tel: 01952 590 005

Fax: 01952 270 962

Helpline: (free) 0808 808 0545

email: ceo@nopanic.co.uk

website: www.nopanic.org.uk

Information and advice for people suffering from panic attacks, obsessive-compulsive disorders, phobias and other related anxiety disorders. Services include a confidential helpline and a night-time anxiety crisis line; teleconferencing CBT (see the case history on page 127); and a six-week one-to-one mentoring scheme. No Panic also provides support for carers and families of sufferers.

First Steps to Freedom

1 Taylor Close

Kenilworth

Warwickshire

CV8 2LW

Tel: 01926 864 473

Fax: 0845 120 2916

Helpline: 0845 120 2916

e-mail: info@first-steps.org

website: www.first-steps.org

Information and advice for people suffering from panic attacks, obsessive-compulsive disorders, phobias and related anxiety disorders. Services include a confidential helpline, telephone self-help groups or one-to-one counselling/befriending and advice and training for people wanting to set up their own helpline or become involved in the First Steps helpline.

The National Phobics Society

Zion Community Resource Centre

339 Stretford Road

Hulme

Manchester

M15 4ZY

Tel: (helpline) 0870 7700 456

Fax: 0161 227 9862

e-mail: nationalphobic@btconnect.com

website: www.phobics-society.org.uk

Charity run by volunteers who have all had experience of anxiety disorders. Aims to help sufferers and campaigns to reduce the stigma associated with mental illness.

MIND (The National Association for Mental Health)

15–19 Broadway

London

E15 4BQ

Tel. 020 8519 2122

Fax: 020 8522 1725

e-mail: contact@mind.org.uk

website: www.mind.org.uk

Promotes needs of people with mental health problems; provides information and advice about mental health issues; and runs more than 200 local MIND associations in England and Wales.

Royal College of Psychiatrists

17 Belgrave Square

London

SW1X 8PG

Tel: 020 7235 2351

email: rcpsych@rcpsych.ac.uk

website: www.rcpsych.ac.uk

Provides mental health information for healthcare professionals and the general public.

Sport England

3rd Floor

Victoria House

Bloomsbury Square

London WC1B 4SE

Tel: 08458 508 508

Fax: 020 7383 5740

email: info@sportengland.org

website: www.sportengland.org.uk

Sport England is committed to creating opportunities for people to start in sport, stay in sport and succeed in sport, and can help you find clubs and activities which are currently running in your area.

The British Dietetic Association

5th Floor

Charles House

148/9 Great Charles Street

Queensway

Birmingham B3 3HT

website: www.bda.uk.com

The BDA is a professional association and this site is intended for its members. The association does, however, have a useful website which includes advice about how to get a dietician as well as dietary information and links to other useful sites.

BBCi

This vast online database holds a wealth of information on healthy living, including diet, exercise and links to resources offering advice on how to improve your quality of life. Questions and answers by the resident expert

on topics including food for mood, with recipes.
website: www.bbc.co.uk/food/healthyeating

Institute of Complementary Medicine

PO Box 194

London

SE16 7QZ

Tel: 020 7237 5165

Fax: 020 7237 5175

e-mail: info@icmedicine.co.uk

website: www.icmedicine.co.uk

The ICM administers the British Register of Complementary Practitioners
(BRCP), a database of registered practitioners in the UK and abroad.

The British Holistic Medical Association

59 Lansdowne Place

Hove

East Sussex

BN3 1FL

Tel/Fax: 01273 725951

e-mail: admin@bhma.org

website: www.bhma.org

The BHMA was formed in 1983 to educate doctors, medical students,
allied health professionals and members of the general public in the
principles and practice of holistic medicine. It is an open membership
association of professionals and members of the public who want to adopt
a more holistic approach in their own life and work.

Further reading

Self Help for your Nerves, Claire Weekes (Thorsons, 1995). Highly acclaimed international guide by the late medical specialist which has been published in many different languages.

Food for Thought, David Benton, (Penguin, 1996). A scientist looks at the evidence about how what we eat affects mood, memory and thinking.

British National Formulary, British Medical Association and the Royal Pharmaceutical Society of Great Britain (September 2004). Guide for doctors listing prescription drugs, their licensed uses, recommended doses and side effects. Regularly updated. Also available on the Internet at www.bnf.org

The South London and Maudsley NHS Trust 2003 Prescribing Guidelines, David Taylor, Carol Paton, Robert Kerwin, (Martin Dunitz, 2003).

Mental Illness: A Handbook for Carers, R. Ramsay, C.Gerada, S. Mars and George Szmukler (Jessica Kingsley, 2001). Written to supply friends and relatives of people who suffer from anxiety disorders with much-needed help and advice.

The Breath Book: Breathe Away Stress, Anxiety and Fatigue with 20 Easy Breathing Techniques, Stella Weller, (HarperCollins, 1999). Proper breathing can calm a racing heart and mind, lower blood pressure, soothe the digestive system, allay anxiety and promote sound sleep. Includes background information on the respiratory system and its link with the heart and circulatory system, as well as exercises to condition the muscles.

Part Two

Useful contacts

British Association for Behavioural and Cognitive Psychotherapists

Globe Centre

PO Box 9

Accrington

BB5 2GD

Tel: 01254 875277

Fax: 01254 239114

email: babcp@babcp.com

website: www.babcp.org.uk

Maintains a register of members who have to present detailed information about training and experience, supported by another qualified practitioner. Bound by ethical standards, including supervision and continuing professional education.

UK Council for Psychotherapy

167–169 Great Portland Street

London

WIN 5PF

Tel: 020 7436 3002

email: ukcp@psychotherapy.org

website: www.psychotherapy.org.uk

Umbrella body with about 90 member organizations representing all main psychotherapeutic traditions. The Royal College of Psychiatrists and the British Psychological Society are represented on the Council.

More than 4,500 (accredited) psychotherapists were registered with the Council in 2003. All accredited therapists train to postgraduate level and agree to conform to the Council's ethical guidelines. The Council sets agreed training criteria for all of its member organizations. There is free access to the register database to find psychotherapists:

- In your local area
- Who practise a particular type of psychotherapy
- Who have wheelchair access
- Who are based outside the UK
- Who belong to a particular member organization.

British Association for Counselling and Psychotherapy
35–37 Albert Street
Rugby
Warwickshire
CV21 2SG
Information line: 0870 443 5252
e-mail: bacp@bacp.co.uk
website: www.bacp.co.uk

Maintains a nationwide directory of accredited private counsellors, plus information on choosing a counsellor. Telephone or send an SAE to above address or use online directory.

Further reading

Living with fear, Isaac Marks (McGraw Hill, 1973). An early book by a medical specialist who is now one of the pioneers of computerized CBT.

Cognitive Therapy and the Emotional Disorders, Aaron T. Beck (Penguin

Books, 1989). The original guide (for both psychotherapists and the general public) by the godfather of cognitive therapy.

Overcoming Panic. A self-help guide using Cognitive Behavioural Techniques, Derrick Silove and Vijaya Manicavasagar (Robinson Publishing, 1997). One of a series of self-help books.

Overcoming Anxiety. A Self-Help Guide Using Cognitive Behavioural Techniques, Helen Kennerley (Robinson Publishing, 1997). One of a series of self-help books.

The Feeling Good Handbook, Dr David Burns (Plume, 1999). A broad-ranging book from US psychiatrist Dr Burns which discusses everything from depression and anxiety, fears and phobias to interpersonal comm-unication and self-esteem.

Mind over Mood, Dennis Greenberger and Christine Padesky (Guilford Press, 1995). Self-help guide by two US clinical psychologists, with the emphasis on case histories, work sheets and practical exercises.

Cognitive Therapy for Depression and Anxiety, Ivy-Marie Blackburn and Kate Davidson, (Blackwell Science Ltd., 1995). Textbook for practitioners by two of the leading British names in the field.

What Works for Whom? A Critical Review of Psychotherapy Research, Anthony Roth and Peter Fonagy (Guilford, 1996). Academic evaluation of research by a clinical psychologist and a psychoanalyst.

Technology in Counselling and Psychotherapy, edited by Stephen Goss and Kate Anthony (Palgrave Macmillan, 2003) Innovative and broad-ranging guide for therapists by a wide range of British and US contributors.

Aimed at professional readership it may be heavy going for the general reader.

Counselling and Psychotherapy: A Consumer's Guide, Windy Dryden and Colin Feltham, (Sheldon Press, 1995). A British response to the ever-increasing demand for "talking therapies".

Computer-aided packages

Beating the Blues: (computerized cognitive behavioural therapy for anxiety and depression). Developed jointly by Ultrasis plc and Dr Judy Proudfoot at the Institute of Psychiatry, King's College, London. Available at some GP surgeries. For more information, go to **www.ultrasis.com** or call **020 7600 6777.**

Restoring the Balance: (Mental Health Foundation, 2000): Based on cognitive behaviour therapy techniques, this CD includes interactive exercises and is designed for people with mild to moderate anxiety or depression. For more information, go to **www.mentalhealth.org.uk** or call **020 7802 0302** during office hours.

Good Days Ahead: Initially designed for use under clinical supervision: a self-help version for home use is now available. Professional actors portray characters overcoming anxiety and depression. For more information go to **www.mindstreet.com** or call **001 502 893 9271**.

FearFighter: Treatment available in the UK via general practitioners. A computer programme to help with anxiety/stress fears, phobias, obsessional behaviour (OCD), post-traumatic stress disorder, nightmares and anger management. Further details can be obtained by either ringing 01384 829124 or e-mailing **stuart@fearfighter.com** or by logging onto

www.fearfighter.com or **www.ccbt.co.uk**. The latter site is designed more for health-care professionals. The English language version of FearFighter is also being used in Europe. There are plans to develop multilingual programmes.

Children

Use Your Brain to Beat Panic and Anxiety is primarily a book for adults. There are several books available which deal specifically with problems of anxiety in children. The following may be useful in helping adults to try and close the gap between themselves and their children with anxiety problems:

Helping Children Cope with Stress, Ursula Markham, Sheldon Press, 1990.

Helping Your Anxious Child, David Lewis, Methuen, 1988.

How to Bring Up Your Child Successfully, Paul Hauck, Sheldon Press, 1982.

Teenagers: The Agony, The Ecstasy, The Answers, Aidan Macfarlane and Ann McPherson (Littlebrown, 1999) covers a wide range of anxiety provoking problems.

Fresher Pressure, also by Macfarlane and McPherson (Oxford University Press, 1994). A guide to life as a student – a time of transition associated with anxiety.

3. Notes to the text

Part One

[1] Villar, R., *Knife Edge: Life as a Special Forces Surgeon*, Michael Joseph,1997.

[2] *WHO Guide to Mental and Neurological Health in Primary Care*, Royal Society of Medicine Press Ltd.

[3] Watts, M. and Cooper, C.L., *Relax. Dealing with Stress*, BBC Books, 1992.

[4] Sheppard, G. *An Aspect of Fear*, Darton, Longman and Todd, 1989.

[5] Holmes, T. and Rahe, R. "The Social Readjustment Rating Scale", *Journal of Psychosomatic Research* 1967; 213–218.

[6] Wallwork, J. and Stepney, R., *Heart Disease: What it is and How it's Treated*, Basil Blackwell, 1987.

[7] Wittchen, H.U., Zhao S., Kessler, R.C., and Eaton, W.W., "Generalized anxiety disorder in the national co-morbidity survey", Archives of *General Psychiatry* 1994; 51: 355–364.

[8] Brown, T.A., Barlow, T.H. and Liebowitz, M.R., "The empirical basis of generalized anxiety disorder", *American Journal of Psychiatry* 1994; 151: 1272–1280.

[9] Kessler, R.C., McGonagle, K.A., Zhao, S., Nelson, C.B., Hughes, M. et al., "Lifetime and 12 month prevalence rates of psychiatric disorders in the USA: Results from the National Co-Morbidity Study " Archives of *General Psychiatry* 1994; 51: 8–19.

[10] Rapoport, J., *The Boy Who Couldn't Stop Washing: the experience and treatment of obsessive-compulsive disorder*, Penguin Group, 1989.

[11] Karno, M. and Golding, J. M., "Obsessive Compulsive Disorder", in Robinson, L.N. and Reiger, D.A.(Eds), *Psychiatric Disorders in America*, New York Free Press, 1994.

[12] Neville, A. *Who's Afraid? Coping with fear, anxiety and panic attacks*, Arrow, l991.

[13] Kessler, R.C., McGonagle, K.A., Zhao, S., Nelson C.B., Hughes M.et al., "Lifetime and 12 month prevalence rates of psychiatric disorders in the USA: Results from the National Co-Morbidity Study", Archives of *General Psychiatry* 1994;51: 8–19.

[14] Ibid.

[15] *World Health Organization Guide to Mental and Neurological Health in Primary Care*, Royal Society of Medicine, 2004.

[16] "Post-traumatic Stress Disorder in a Community Sample", Brian Engdahl et al, *American Journal of Psychiatry*, 1997, pages 1576–81

[17] Swinson, R.P., Soulios C., Cox B.J., Kunch K., "Brief treatment of emergency room patients with panic attacks", *American Journal of Psychiatry* 1992; 149: 944–946.

[18] *World Health Organisation Guide to Mental and Neurological Health in Primary Care*, second edition, Royal Society of Medicine, 2004.

[19] Hirschfield, R., "The Co-morbidity of Major Depression and Anxiety Disorders: Recognition and Management in Primary Care", *Primary Care Companion, Journal of Clinical Psychiatry* 2001; 3: 244–254.

[20] National Institute for Clinical Excellence, UK, "Guidance on the Use of Computerized Behavioural Therapy for Anxiety and Depression", *Technology Appraisal Guide* No. 51, October 2002.

[21] Ashton, C.H., *Benzodiazepines: how they Work and How to Withdraw*, www. benzo.org.uk

[22] Tyrer, P, *How to Stop Taking Tranquillizers*, Sheldon Press, 1986.

[23] Burns, D., *The Feeling Good Handbook*, Plume, 1999.

[24] Eisenberg, D. M., Davis, R., Ettner, S. L. et al. "Trends in alternative medicine use in the United States, 1990–1997", *Journal of the American Medical Association* 1998; 280: 1569–1575.

[25] Ernst, E. et al., *The Desk Top Guide to Complementary and Alternative Medicine*. Mosby, 2001.

[26] Astin J.A., "Stress reduction through mindfulness meditation. Effects on psychological symptomatology, sense of control and spiritual experiences", *Psychotherapy Psychosomatics*, 1997; 66: 97–106.

[27] Gift, A.G., Moore, T. and Soeken, K., "Relaxation to reduce dyspnea and anxiety in COPD patients", 1992; 41: 242–246.

[28] Breslow, L. and Enstrom, J.E., "Persistence of health habits and their relationship to mortality." *Preventive Medicine* 1980; 9: 469–483. (NB: Reports in the 1990s indicate that the good effects reported earlier continued to persist.)

[29] Dudley, E., *Run for your life*, Columbus Books, 1985.

[30] Rippe, J.M., *Fit for Success: Proven Strategies for Executive Health*, Prentice Hall Press, 1989.

[31] Adapted from *Food for Thought*, David Benton, Penguin Books, 1996.

Part Two

[1] Goleman, D., *Vital Lies, Simple Truths. The Psychology of Self-Deception*, Bloomsbury, 1997.

[2] Bennett, G., *Patients and their Doctors*, Secker and Warburg, l979.

[3] Newman, M.G., "The Clinical Use of Palmtop Computers in the Treatment of Generalized Anxiety Disorder", *Cognitive and Behavioural Practice* 1999; 6: 222–234.

[4] Dobson, R., "GPs prescribe self-help books or mental health problems", *British Medical Journal* 2003; 326: 1285.

[5] Smith, N. M., Floyd, M.R., Jamison, C. and Scogin, F., "Three year follow-up of bibliotherapy for depression", *Journal of Consulting and Clinical Psychology* 1997; 65: (2) 324–327.

[6] Contributor, *Changing Minds. Our Lives and Mental Illness.* Edited by Rosalind Ramsay, Ann Page, Tricia Goodman and Deborah Hart, Royal College of Psychiatrists, Gaskell, 2002.

[7] Roth, A., Fonagy, P., *What Works for Whom? A Critical Review of Psychotherapy Research,* The Guilford Press, 1996.

[8] Durham, R.C., Murphy T., Allan T., Richard, K., Treliving L.R. and Fenton, G.W., "Cognitive therapy, analytic psychotherapy and anxiety management training for generalised anxiety disorder", *British Journal of Psychiatry* 1994; 165: 315–323.

[9] Sheppard, G. *An Aspect of Fear,* Darton, Longman and Todd, 1989.

Part Three

[1] Taylor, D., Paton, C., and Kerwin, R., *The Maudsley: The South London and Maudsley NHS Trust 2003 Prescribing Guidelines 7th edition,* Martin Dunitz, 2003.

[2] Bond, A. and Lader, M., *Understanding Drug Treatment in Mental Health Care,* John Wiley and Sons, 1996.

[3] Ibid.

[4] Lejeoyeux, M., Ades, J., Mourad, I., "Antidepressant withdrawal syndrome: recognition, prevention and managements", *CNS Drugs,* 1996; 5: 278–292.

[5] Lacey R., *The Complete Guide to Psychiatric Drugs: A Layman's Handbook,* Ebury Press, 1991.

[6] *British National Formulary No. 46,* September 2003.

[7] Bond, A. and Lader, M., *Understanding Drug Treatment in Mental Health Care,* John Wiley and Sons, 1996.

[8] Cantopher, T., *Depressive Illness. The curse of the strong,* Sheldon Press, 2003.

[9] Mendels, J., Krajewski, T.F., Huffer, V. et al. "Effective Short Term Treatment of generalized anxiety with trifluoperazine", *Journal of Clinical Psychiatry,* 1986; 47: 170–174.

[10] "Best treatments", NHS Direct, in association with Clinical Evidence, BMJ Publishing Group, 2004.

[11] Van Harten, P.N., Hoek, H.W., Matroos, G.E. et al. "Intermittent neuroleptic treatment and risk for tardive dykinesia: Curacco Extrapyramidal Syndromes Study 111", *American Journal of Psychiatry,* 1998; 155: (4) 565–567

[12] Taylor, D., Paton C., and Kerwin, R., *The South London and Maudsley NHS Trust 2003 Prescribing Guidelines 7th edition,* Martin Dunitz, 2003.

[13] Burns, D., *The Feeling Good Handbook,* Plume, 1999.

Permissions

Page 16 "Anxiety checklist". From the WHO Guide to Mental and Neurological Health in Primary Care, Royal Society of Medicine Press Ltd. Reprinted with permission of Professor Rachel Jenkins, Director, WHO Collaborating Centre, and Head of Section of Mental Health Policy, Institute of Psychiatry, King's College London.

Page 19 "Locus of Control" questionnaire from *Relax: Dealing With Stress* by Murray Watts and Professor Cary L. Cooper, published by BBC Books. Reproduced by permission of Professor Cooper who based the questionnaire on a scale devised by Julian Rotter in 1966.

Page 27 "Human Performance Curve" from *The Complete Guide to Stress Management* by Dr Chandra Patel, published by Vermillion. Used by permission of The Random House Group Limited.

Page 124 Palmtop computer chart. Reproduced with the permission of Dr Michelle Newman, director of the Center for the Treatment of Anxiety and Depression, Department of Psychology, Pennsylvania State University. Dr Newman wishes to acknowledge the contributions of Justin Kenardy, Steve Herman and Barr Taylor.

Publisher's acknowledgements

The publisher gratefully acknowledges the permission granted to reproduce the copyright material in this book. Every effort has been made to trace the copyright holders and to obtain permission for the use of copyright material. The publisher apologizes for any errors or omissions and would be grateful if notified of any corrections that should be incorporated in future reprints or editions of the book.

4. Picture credits

p.12 John Foxx/ Alamy; p.15 Scott Camazine/ Science Photo Library; p.23 Bsip Alexandre/ Science Photo Library; p.38 Cristina Pedrazzini/ Science Photo Library; p.42 (top) Zakwaters/ Alamy, (middle) Steve Horrell/ Science Photo Library, (bottom) Harvey Twyman/ Alamy; p. 50 (top) Novosti/ Science Photo Library; p. 52 Wellcome Dept. of Cognitive Neurology/ Science Photo Library; p.58 Cordelia Molloy/ Science Photo Library; p.68 Kai Chiang/ Superstock/ Alamy; p.71 Lawrence Lawry/ Science Photo Library; p.75 Bsip Collet/ Science Photo Library; p. 84 (top) P. Hattenberger, Publiphoto diffusion/ Science Photo Library, (bottom) Matthew Munro/ Science Photo Library; p.94 Photo Researchers/ Science Photo Library; p. 109 Banana Stock/Alamy; p. 120 Luca DiCecco/Alamy; p. 121 Lawrence Lawry/ Science Photo Library

5. Bibliography

American Psychiatric Association, *Diagnostic and Statistical Manual of Mental Disorders* (4th edition), 1994.

Beck, A., *Cognitive Therapy and the Emotional Disorders*, Penguin Books, 1989.

Bennett, G.,*Patients and their Doctors*, Secker and Warburg, 1979.

Benton, D., *Food for Thought*, Penguin, 1996.

Blackburn, I.M., Davidson, K., *Cognitive Therapy for Depression and Anxiety*, Blackwell Science, 1995.

Bond, A.J., Lader, M.J., *Understanding Drug Treatment in Mental Health*, Wiley, 1996.

Breton, S., *Panic Attacks. A Practical Guide to Recognizing and Dealing with Feelings of Panic*, Vermillion, 1996.

British Medical Association and the Royal Pharmaceutical Society of Great Britain, *British National Formulary*, September 2003.

Burns, D., *The Feeling Good Handbook*, Plume, 1999.

Cabe, J., *Understanding Tranquillizer Use: The Role of the Social Sciences*, Routledge, 1991.

Carter, R., *Consciousness*, Weidenfeld and Nicolson, 2001.

Carter, R., *Mapping the Mind*, Phoenix, 1998.

Costa, E. (editor), *The Benzodiazepines. From Molecular Biology to Clinical Practice*, Raven Press, 1983.

Davison, G., Neale, J. M., *Abnormal Psychology*, Wiley, 1998.

Dryden, W., Feltham, C., *Counselling and Psychotherapy. A Consumer's Guide*, Sheldon Press, 1995.

Ernst, E. et al, *Desktop Guide to Complementary and Alternative Medicine, An Evidence Based Approach*, Mosby, 2001.

Eysenck, H.J., *Psychology is about People*, Allen Lane, The Penguin Press, 1972.

Goleman, D.,*Vital Lies, Simple Truths: The Psychology of Self-Deception*, Bloomsbury, 1997.

Goss, S., Anthony, K., (editors), *Technology in Counselling and Psychotherapy, A Practitioner's Guide*, Palgrave Macmillan, 2003.

Greenburger, D., Padesky, C., *Mind Over Mood*, Guilford Press, 1995.

Harvey, S., Wylie, I., *Patient Power*, Simon & Schuster, 1999.

Ingham, C., *Panic Attacks*, Thorsons, 1993.

Kennerley, H., *Overcoming Anxiety. A Self-Help Guide using Cognitive Behavioural Techniques*, Robinson Publishing, 1997.

Kiley, R., Graham, E., *The Patient's Internet Handbook*, Royal Society of Medicine Press, 2001.

Lacey, R., *The Complete Guide to Psychiatric Drugs: A Layman's Handbook*, Ebury Press, 1991.

Macfarlane, A., McPherson, A., *Fresher Pressure: How to Survive as a Student*, Oxford Paperbacks, 1994.

Mark, J., Williams, G., *Treatment of Depression: A Guide to the Theory and Practice of Cognitive Behaviour Therapy*, Routledge, 1992.

Maud, V., *Stress and Depression in Children and Teenagers*, Sheldon Press, 2002.

Michelson, L., Ascher, L. (editors)

Anxiety and Stress Disorders, Cognitive-Behavioural Assessment and Treatment, Guilford Press, 1987.

Morrison, A. L., *A User's Guide for Patients and Families, The Antidepressant Sourcebook*, Main Street Books, Doubleday, 2000.

Morton, I., Hall, J., J. Halliday, (consultants), *Tranquillizers. The Comprehensive Guide*, Bloomsbury, 1992.

Neville, A., *Who's Afraid? Coping with Fear, Anxiety and Panic Attack*, Arrow Books, 1991.

Patel, C., *The Complete Guide To Stress Management*, Vermillion, 1996.

Persaud R., *Staying Sane*, Metro, 1997.

Ramsay, R., Page A., Goodman T., and Hart, D. (editors), *Changing Minds: Our Lives and Mental Illness*, Gaskell, 2002.

Ramsay, R., Gerada, C., Mars, S., Szmukler, G., *Mental Illness: A Handbook for Carers*, Jessica Kingsley, 2001.

Rippe, J.M., *Fit for Success. Proven Strategies for Executive Health*, Prentice Hall Press, 1989.

Roth, A., Fonagy, P., *What Works for Whom? A Critical Review of Psychotherapy Research*, Guilford, 1996.

Royal Society of Medicine Press, *World Health Organization Guide to Mental and Neurological Health in Primary Care*, 2004.

Selye, H., *Stress without Distress*, Lippincott and Crowell, 1974.

Sheppard, G., *An Aspect of Fear*, Darton, Longman and Todd, 1989.

Silove, D. and Manicavasagar, V.,

Overcoming Panic A Self Help Guide Using Cognitive Behavioural Techniques, Robinson Publishing, 1997.

Stern R. S., Drummond, L..M., *Treatment of Depression. Practice of Behavioural and Cognitive Psychotherapy*, Cambridge University Press, 1991.

Sutherland, S., *Breakdown: A Personal Crisis and a Medical Dilemma*, Oxford University Press, 1998.

Taylor, D., Paton, C., Kerwin, R., *The South London and Maudsley NHS Trust 2003 Prescribing Guidelines*, Martin Dunitz, 2003.

Texas Heart Institute, *Heart Owner's Handbook*, John Wiley and Sons, Inc., 1996.

Totman, R., *Mind, Stress and Health*, Souvenir Press, 1990.

Trickett, S., *Coping with Anxiety and Depression*, Sheldon Press, 1989.

Tyrer Peter, *How to Stop Taking Tranquillizers*, Sheldon Press, 1986.

Vines, R., *Agoraphobia. The Fear of Panic*, Fontana, 1987.

Watkins, A. (editor), *Mind Body Medicine: A Clinician's Guide to Psychoneuroimmunology*, Churchill Livingstone, 1997.

Watts, M., Cooper, C.L., *Relax. Dealing with Stress*, BBC Books, 1992.

Wood, C., *Living in Overdrive*, Fontana, 1984.

Wootton, R., Yellowlees, P., McClaren, P., *Telepsychiatry and e-Mental Health*, Royal Society of Medicine Press, 2003.

6. Index